THE TRIATHLON TRAINING AND RACING BOOK

THE
TRIATHLON
TRAINING AND RACING
BOOK

SALLY EDWARDS

CONTEMPORARY
BOOKS, INC.
CHICAGO

Library of Congress Cataloging in Publication Data

Edwards, Sally.
    The triathlon training and racing book.

    Includes index.
    1. Triathlon—Training—Addresses, essays, lectures.
    2, Athletes—Biography—Addresses, essays, lectures.
    I. Title.
GV1060.7.E385   1985   796.4′092′2 [B]   85-3801
ISBN 0-8092-5430-1

Published by Contemporary Books, Inc.
180 North Michigan Avenue, Chicago, Illinois 60601
Manufactured in the United States of America
Library of Congress Catalog Card Number: 85-3801
International Standard Book Number: 0-8092-5430-1

Published simultaneously in Canada by Beaverbooks, Ltd.
195 Allstate Parkway, Valleywood Business Park
Markham, Ontario L3R 4T8 Canada

CONTENTS

PREFACE

The inspiration for this book arrived in the mail one day. Someone wanted more information about triathlons after reading my first book, *Triathlon: A Triple Fitness Sport*. She was curious about the top triathletes—how they train and race, what their daily routines are. She wanted to know what they eat, think, and feel.

With that prodding, I decided a book would be worth writing, but only if it were compelling and made a real contribution to the sport. To do that, it would have to fulfill three criteria: be inspirational, explain the tools of multisport fitness (mental and physical), and tell the personal stories of the top triathletes.

The first questions that arose about the book concerned its format. After reading interviews in every major publication, I decided that the most authentic format would be to let the triathletes tell their own stories. You will be reading the words they spoke, sensing the way they felt. Perhaps you will be able to read into their words the texture of their voices, the dimensions of their personalities, the way they view their training and racing, and, of course, their use of the tools of success.

The triathletes selected the tools or mechanisms they felt they used most effectively. They then told, in first-person singular, the threefold accounts.

- their personal stories;
- their personal experiences using the tool or mechanism;
- their personal training schedules and racing strategies.

A major focus of my interview was how each triathlete used the identifiable attributes of success. I also sought the underlying motivations: Why do triathletes do what they do, and what do they earn and learn from it? Through this approach, I hope you discover the bond—the tools and the mechanisms—that all successful athletes share.

In reading the book, you will quickly note that there are few obvious similarities among these athletes; their differences seem far more substantial. Yet in their quests to win, each of them has realized a common truth: what motivates them to compete is not a drive for fame or material gain but a passion to do their best. At the root of this passion that compels them to improve continually lies a vision of excellence that each of them strives to transform into reality.

These pages are for you to reflect upon; they should not be adopted as gospel. No one else is exactly like you, so take any information you discover here and use it to become stronger than you were before, yet remain a free-thinking individual.

I want to thank each of these triathletes for the cooperation and time they gave to express their views on training and their attitudes toward the sport. I know that they did this not to boast of their accomplishments but to relate their own experience in order to help others.

1
THE DEFINITIONS
STAR, CHAMPION, HERO, LEGEND

A young Indian brave from Kansas ran across the Century 21 movie screen in Sacramento, California. Here in his adopted hometown, where the film was first released, no one was in the audience. The entire theater was empty, every seat vacant. After waiting and planning for 20 years, Olympic gold medal winner Billy Mills had the opportunity for a smashing major motion picture. It became his challenge. He had rejected offers of television movies and specials about him. Billy had his own vision of the way his movie should be done.

His is the story of an American Indian boy raised on a reservation by his sister—a story of poverty, loneliness, suicide, and despair. He wanted it to be told in the Billy Mills way. He wanted the portrait of raw athletic talent, the conflict between the white and red cultures, and the 10,000-meter race in which he won the Olympic gold medal to express the special meanings he had found in each of them. His hope was to portray a star who became a champion, then a hero; his dream was to metamorphose that hero into a living legend.

The Billy Mills story brings tears to our eyes. Off the screen, Billy Mills is charismatic, powerful. His openness and concern for the plight of North America's real pioneers—the Indian nations—demands admiration. But the step from admiration to inspiration was taken when a dark horse athlete's championship performance made him a true hero.

The difference between a star and a champion may seem oblique—both are winners. But a star wins for the glory of self, while a champion wins for a greater glory: for team, family, country, or sport. A champion doesn't merely win a contest, he or she sets standards of excellence that are measured by time or distance.

A hero is even more special than a champion. It is on the shoulders of our heroes that our hearts and hopes are carried onto the playing field. They give us reason to believe that we too can reach beyond the apparent limits of our daily lives and find the heroes in ourselves. Because we look up to them, they seem bigger than life.

When you first meet Scott Molina, for example, you might be surprised to find that he is of such small physical stature. He seems so much larger when he rises out of the water like a fearless gladiator, defeating all competition. Week after week, race after race, Scott tests himself and his competitors, pushing new limits in all three triathlon sports. Scott Molina is a hero because he paves the way not just for himself but also for his peers, challenging them to outperform him, to swim, cycle, and run faster than they've ever had to before.

Consider the specific athletes of the triathlon sports. The swimmers are seen as the silent ones, keeping their noses clean and in the pool. Though the drama of a 200-yard backstroke may be less apparent than a touchdown at the Super Bowl, some swimmers have bucked those 20th-century odds to attain all four levels of success: from star to champion to hero to legend.

Winning one gold medal at the 1976 Olympics would have made Mark Spitz a star, but in becoming the first American ever to win four at once, he shook the most sedentary spectators from their sofas and established himself as a champion. His fame and fortune have been a yardstick of that success.

The heroes, however, are athletes such as marathon swimmer Diana Nyad. She went beyond the boundaries of a pool, accomplishing what had once seemed impossible—a swim from the border of Cuba to the United States—and inspiring others to test themselves at tasks in their own lives that might seem equally impossible.

But swimmers like Donna DeVerona are the true legends, because their successes and challenges extend beyond the world of sports to efforts that make each of our lives richer. After she proved her mettle in swimming by becoming an Olympic multiple-medalist at age 16, Donna tested her leadership in politics and the media by directing her energy at the Women's Sports Foundation, of which she is president, and at broadcasting for ABC Sports, of which she is a vice president.

That is the difference between heroes and legends. Though we admire and respect heroes, the contributions that legends make to the world at large live on far beyond their lifetimes. For that reason, some people believe that legends cannot be designated as such until their lives have ended. On the contrary, the legends who serve us best are those who are very much alive, whose lives we can relate to our own.

If Dave Scott were a name from the past, a figure out of ancient history, his domination of triathlon's most infamous race—the Hawaii Ironman—would be a subject for idle conversation rather than an ongoing challenge to top-level triathletes and an inspiration to the rest. The fact that Dave is alive and well and still competing is a testament not only to his own endurance as a champion but also to that of the sport itself. When he entered his first Ironman, triathlons were considered a bizarre novelty event for a handful of faddists; aided by the media exposure and word-of-mouth publicity that world-class athletes have brought to it, the sport has endured and grown—and Dave Scott is still toeing the starting line.

Now take a look at cyclists. Though Jacques "Jock" Boyer was the first American to ride the Tour de France, he remains relatively obscure. While his accomplishment did not go entirely unnoticed, neither did it inspire Little Leaguers to abandon the batting cage for a future on the road.

John Howard, a three-time Olympian who has been called the best cyclist of his generation, embodies the spark, the vision, that makes a hero out of a star. Sport is a vehicle for John's limitless imagination, a stepping stone toward a more complete self. He is an adventurer, a pioneer. He was one of the first "Ironmen," one of the first to race his bicycle nonstop from "sea to shining sea," and he continues to seek new frontiers, just as he continues to break bike course records in nearly every triathlon he enters.

But in the world of pure cycling, American heroes have been relatively scarce. The first American truly to challenge the imperious Europeans at their own game was Greg LeMond, the first U.S. native to take the world championship (1983). With the support of the right team, LeMond could also dress an American in the yellow winner's jersey at the Tour de France—another first. The three-week-plus stage race is considered the most arduous bicycle race in the world, as well as one of the most challenging overall endurance contests.

In America, though, the most commonly shared symbol of hope and possibility in the athletic world is probably the runner. The legends are many, from Jesse Owens' masterful performances that upstaged Nazi Germany's pompousness and bigotry in Berlin (1936) to Wilma Rudolph's strength and grace, which brought confidence to an entire generation of women. Because the running boom has introduced the sport into the lives of millions of Americans, many people have enjoyed one-shot opportunities to become stars, but that has not detracted from the special value of our champions—people like marathon world record holders Joan Benoit and Alberto Salazar.

Running has delivered its share of heroes. We cheered for Mary Decker at the 1983 World Championships in Helsinki when she broke the tape inches in front of the Russians, who collapsed at the finish, just as we cried with her when she fell at the Olympics. But it was in 1972 that Frank Shorter truly advanced the sport. He thrust his bony shoulders across the Olympic marathon finish line tape in a gold medal performance.

Frank's previous running deeds had already made him a star; his gold medal made him a champion. Now, years later, his continuing battle for excellence against the odds is symbolic of his heroism. His continued efforts to encourage each of us become fit have made him a legend. Rather than the memory of his deeds fading, his legend has grown.

You will have to decide for yourself how each of the triathletes represented in this book should be classified; star, champion, hero, or legend. Some are still on the up side of their careers, others are champions, setting new levels of performance. Fewer still are heroes, leading us to places we have never gone before, places we could once only dream of. And some might be living legends.

Who are you?

All of us are at least stars unto ourselves. Given, then, that you are in the family of athletes and people who recognize their own self-worth, can you envision yourself as a champion, hero, or legend?

These pages tell the tales of triathletes who understand and practice some or all of the five tools and five mechanisms of success in athletics. These winning attributes apply not only to athletics but to all aspects of your life as you change from a shining star to a living legend to your friends, family, and/or, if you choose, to your generation and the ones that follow. It is up to you to make such decisions, to accomplish your goals, and to become whatever you wish to be.

It is a metamorphic process, an application of the sports metaphor. Take the lead and serve as a living model. By changing ourselves we can change our society and make it a place of success rather than failure.

Every aspiring triathlete knows that there is always room for improvement. Triathletes know that there is always room at the top. They know that they can learn from others. Consequently, they want to know how the stars train, what the champions do, why the

THE TOOLS AND MECHANISMS OF SUCCESS

ATTITUDINAL TOOLS	TRIATHLETE	VALUE MECHANISMS	TRIATHLETE
1. Incurable Optimism:	Scott Tinley	⟶ 1. Burning Desire:	Scott Molina
2. Limitless Imagination:	John Howard	⟶ 2. Blind Focus:	Sylviane and Patricia Puntous
3. Decisive Control:	Mark Allen	⟶ 3. Addictive Discipline:	Linda Buchanan
4. Deep-Down Confidence:	Julie Moss	⟶ 4. Double-Win Spirit:	Ardis Bow
5. Keen Awareness:	David F. Scott	⟶ 5. Vivacious Strength:	Kurt Madden

heroes are admired, and at what point the legends emerge.

The quest and thirst for information is just one of the processes involved in the improvement cycle. A more important process is for the triathlete to become a constantly improving performer. To do so means implementing the information and then interpreting the results accurately. But in a world that continues to process more and more information and to produce more and more legends, is there a simple way to do this?

When the sports psychologists and exercise physiologists, ergometric researchers, nutritionists, and psychiatrists try to discover why two identical athletes perform so unequally, the same reasons are uncovered. As the ingredients of winning are identified, they are always reduced to the same basic keys or tools, the same processes or mechanisms. Though triathletes display varying amounts of each, they use them in different ways. The important point is that all successful athletes use all of the tools and all the mechanisms to one degree or another.

Access to the five tools and five mechanisms is gained sequentially. As you become more adept at one winning quality, you discover how to use it. The process continues as you head toward the total winning attitude. This is much more than psychology. It is the very real creation of a successful lifestyle, one that is inspiring to you and simultaneously a healthy example to others who seek your guidance and positive encouragement.

Each of these triathletes provides three services in this book: they explain their training programs to us, they share their racing experiences, and they reveal their secrets. They have integrated the parts—the tools and the mechanisms—into a whole program that works successfully for them and that you can understand.

2
TOOL 1
INCURABLE OPTIMISM

After swimming 2.4 miles, I found it difficult to walk up the ramp without tottering. This was 1981, my first Ironman Triathlon. Between the ramp and the finish line remained a 112-mile bicycle race and a 26.2-mile run. But I felt optimistic; I knew I would finish the race.

Of the 300-plus bicycles that had been aligned in perfect order in the swim-to-bike transition area, only a few were still standing—the bike storage area was virtually deserted. I was almost in last place. But, assessing the situation and knowing that opportunities in life often disguise themselves as problems, I vowed to pass as many of my competitors as possible.

By the end of the 112-mile bike race, I had moved forward a hundred places and my confidence had grown in proportion to my progress. As I started the marathon, I was the 10th-place woman, and I knew that I would pass most of the runners ahead. To know, in that sense, was an act of faith. It was a feeling rather than a proven fact. I believed my positive feeling; my inner voice reinforced my optimism.

One at a time, I passed the runners ahead of me. I would imagine myself snagging a competitior and then reeling her in—catching one fish after another. There was, however, one fish I didn't catch—Linda Sweeney. Linda won first place that year. I finished second.

The experience of winning in athletic contests becomes a tool that you can use over and over again to recreate success. During the 1981 Ironman race, I expected to win; in fact, I had armed myself with one of the five tools of winning—incurable optimism—in spite of the doubts of friends and associates back home in Sacramento, California.

To eliminate luck or to take the gamble out of sports, successful athletes link their physical skills with their mental strengths. In successful performance, there is a direct correlation between a person's body and a person's mind. Academicians call it *psychosomatic aptitude.* Simply stated, your body affects your mind, and your mind affects your body. This can be seen most clearly in medicine. Physicians know that our bodies are exposed to and carry germs, yet only infrequently do we become ill. Avoiding disease depends upon how effectively our immune system can repel the attacking germs. Winning athletes develop a mental immune system that produces psychic antibodies to defend against intrusion from germs, especially those that carry "diseases" such as negative stress, hyperanxiety, and the fear of losing.

Champions use this mind/body relationship in other ways as well. They know it is possible to actualize an obsessive desire, to become whatever they imagine themselves to be. Champions are what they expect to be—champions. Though they may not always get what they deserve—nor deserve what they get—champions know that ultimately they will get what they *expect* to get. True mental immunity reinforces a person's sense of incurable optimism.

Winning athletes believe that they will win. They know that winning, by definition, is performing to their maximum mental and physical ability, not just crossing the finishing line first. Winning is personal excellence; losing is focusing on the penalties of failure rather than on the rewards of victory. Losers expect to be injured or that the water will be cold; their pessimism leads them to rely on luck to win. Winners eliminate the gamble by taking three positive approaches to competition:

1. Preparation: In training, winners practice both the mental and the physical skills necessary to win.
2. Self-control: Winning athletes know that they are responsible for their success, and they make it happen.
3. Desire: Winners feed their hunger for victory with daily "meals" of winning.

Incurable optimism reflects the athlete's ability to create success in his or her mind. Without a dream, the other tools of success are useless. A champion has no room for pessimism. My own experience in the 1981 Ironman Triathlon illustrates the incurably optimis-

Roger Allyn Lee

Running across the finish line: Receiving a flower lei and smiling are Sally Edwards' trademarks.

tic condition. As I approached the finish line, the streets were crowded with jubilant spectators. Their personal passion for victory helped fuel those final steps, yet every triathlete knew that the race was a self-fulfilling prophecy. We knew before we started that we would finish—we were incurably afflicted with optimism. And we have come to realize that the finish line of any race is the start of yet another.

SCOTT PATRICK TINLEY

Hometown: San Diego
Date of birth: October 25, 1956
Height: 6'0"
Weight: 155 pounds
Maximum VO$_2$: 78 ml/kg/min on treadmill
Body fat: 7 percent
Current profession: Professional athlete/marketing associate, sports entrepreneur

Athletic achievements:

1982: Bud Light Ironman, first-place
1983: Bud Light Ironman, second place
1984: U.S.T.S. Atlanta, tied for first place
Midwest Classic, first place (world record for Ironman distance)

Scott Tinley, a man afflicted with incurable optimism.

FROM SURFER TO IRONMAN:
THE GROWTH OF AN OPTIMIST

I was born in Santa Monica (greater Los Angeles) in 1956. My parents were very athletic, especially in water sports; they didn't swim competitively, but they loved to surf and sail. There are eight children in my family—seven by my first father, one by my step-father. My dad died from cancer when I was 15, so we seven kids had to survive without him. He had been very unselfish in spending time with us when we were young and had given up a lot of potential athletic achievements of his own for us.

In my childhood, I had the classic Little League background. My eye/hand coordination is fair, so I played third base on the baseball team. As a child, I lacked any kind of formal training in swimming, which is a shame, because it would have made a lot of difference in my triathlon performance. Being able to swim well is one of the biggest challenges in my athletic career. I now swim 25,000 yards a week, and it's all quality stuff.

My high school was extremely football-oriented because a football program supported it. The team was number one in the state for several years in a row. As a freshman, I probably played about three minutes during the entire season. I got my butt kicked, and I hated it, but I never quit. One of my greatest athletic strengths is not quitting.

Our school also had a weightlifting program that everybody—especially the football players—had to go through. But between my freshman and sophomore years, I injured my back doing a flip on the trampoline, so I couldn't lift for three weeks. Pressured by my peers—they'd say, "Well, go run, shrimp"—I started running around the track. I would do four or five miles. That probably marked the beginning of my development in aerobic fitness and in specific running training. That year I went out for cross-country, and within six weeks I was doing very well, expecially on the trails and hills. In track, I ran high 4:40s in the mile and comparable times in the two-mile. Senioritis struck after that, and I developed other interests.

In college, I got into tennis and played well for about two years, even participating in tournaments, but it wasn't until I moved to San Diego in 1976 that I really found my niche. I lived with a Japanese friend who hung out at the beach. We weren't into athletics then; we just worked and went to school. It was my roommate's father who really brought about the change. He was 58 and could run a 3:05 marathon. He said to us, "Look at the life you live" and he bet us we couldn't finish the marathon in under four hours and gave us six weeks to train. We both broke out the old leather Adidas Cortez. Thanks to that man's incentive, I ran a 3:18 and my friend just broke four hours. After the race, we stuck with it.

Since then, I've stopped running only once, for six months, when I was a member of the crew team at San Diego State. I loved rowing, not only because it was an aquatic sport but also because it has some great aesthetic qualities. I enjoyed getting up at 5:00 A.M. and rowing on the bay just as the sun was coming up. As far as general fitness is concerned, rowing is a lot like the triathlon because it builds upper-body strength and develops cardiovascular fitness. If it weren't for the fact that I don't like team sports, I would have continued rowing.

After I graduated I entered paramedic school, then worked as a paramedic for a year and as a firefighter for six months. It was in the summer of 1980 that I first trained seriously, because as a fireman with 24-hour shifts I had plenty of time off, working 10 days a month with 4 or 5 days off in a row, once a month. I would

Dave Epperson

do plenty of bike riding and running but very little swimming, tying my training in with my job. (I didn't know how to swim well; 1,500 yards was a tough workout for me.) I'd team up with men who were also into athletics. While waiting for calls, we would run 10–12 miles around a 1-mile park. We couldn't do anything overly strenuous because we didn't want to pass out on a call, but we'd get a fair amount of training done on duty; we'd even swim in the afternoons.

But I couldn't imagine being a fireman for the rest of my life, so in 1981 I returned to the San Diego Aquatic Center and assumed a lot of administrative responsibility. The change was a big blow to my training because I worked a 50-hour week. Inevitably, my training suffered.

I first realized my potential as a triathlete when I came in third at the 1981 Ironman. I had entered hoping simply to finish. I rode a 25-inch SR Grand Course bicycle that probably weighed 28 pounds. In the tool kit for my bike I had vise grips, big screwdrivers, an eight-inch crescent wrench, heavy clinchers, and touring shoes. I raced in a baggy singlet. As you can see, I wasn't exactly sophisticated, but I completed the event in 10 hours, 12 minutes. I began to get more serious about triathlons after that, and for about two years I worked full-time and went to night school to get my master's degree. I knew if I left school I would never go back. Taking nine units of graduate courses, I had to train before work, during my lunchtime, and between work and school. I was going crazy.

In the summer of '81, it became possible to participate in more than three triathlons in San Diego County. That was the first year of the Horny Toad Triathlon, and I went up and did a race in Santa Barbara, one in Davis, and a few others here and there. That summer I won four races and felt really confident. Also, I had married Virginia, whom I met at the Aquatic Center. She had become a stewardess and had been flying out of Chicago and Cleveland for three years. In the fall, I started training a little harder. I decided I would do the Ironman one more year (it was then February) to see what I could do with more experience. That was 1982, the year I won. Once you win you can never quit. You have a tiger by the tail, but it's also got you.

A lot of changes were happening in my life then. For another year I worked at the Aquatic Center and worked on my master's degree; but finally, I realized I couldn't do everything. School was the first thing to go. I took long (two-hour) lunches to train, but that wasn't fair to the people I worked with, so I gave up the Aquatic Center in the late fall of 1982. Team J. David contacted me about that time. I accepted the J. David offer and worked at a part-time position at Second Sole in promotions. I had to do something at least three days a week—I need to work mentally as well as physically.

TINLEY'S TRAINING:
A RELENTLESS REHEARSAL
OF OPTIMISM

I don't think I'm mature enough yet to develop a year-round program, because I can't take more than two days off without feeling guilty. So I usually follow a weekly training schedule; the

Dave Epperson

Scott started as a runner and found triathlons his forte.

races follow one another so closely that there is really no off-season, anyway. My average weekly mileage is 25,000–30,000 yards in swimming, 400–450 miles on the bike, and 70–80 miles of running. In the past year, I've had only six days off. I think I come somewhere between Scott Molina's average of 500 miles a week on the bike (at 17 mph) and Mark Allen's average of 250 miles (at 22 mph).

Because I do a lot more than just train, I have had to learn how to use my time efficiently. I work 15 hours a week in the office and another 10 just answering letters and making phone calls. I don't allow myself excuses. A lot of people say they can't train because they have no time, but I try to make time by combining my more mundane activities. For example, I often eat while I'm driving. I have developed a schedule based on the amount of time I have available, and I work only on Monday, Wednesday, and Friday afternoons.

My program on Monday is fairly typical for me. I have breakfast before I leave in the morning. First I ride between the hours of 8:15 and 11:45 A.M. Monday is usually speed-work day: 50 intervals

SCOTT TINLEY'S TYPICAL WEEKLY SCHEDULE

	SWIMMING	BIKING	RUNNING	WEIGHTS
MONDAY	12:00–1:30 P.M.: 4,800–5,000 yards	8:15–11:45 A.M.: speed work	5:30–6:30 P.M.: 6–7½ miles	30–40 minutes
TUESDAY	4:30–6:00 P.M.	10:00–3:00 P.M.	8:00–9:30 A.M.: quality hill run, 12–14 miles, *or* intervals, mile repeats on a trail	
WEDNESDAY	Repeat Monday	Easy ride	Repeat Monday	30–40 minutes
THURSDAY	4:30–6:00 P.M.: repeat Tuesday	Repeat Tuesday	Run track *or* intervals, hill repeats	
FRIDAY	Repeat Monday	Repeat Monday	7–9 miles	30–40 minutes
SATURDAY	Postbike swim: very easy 1,000–1,500 yards	Postrun ride: 100 miles	Fast, continuous morning run or a 10k	
SUNDAY	Postrun swim: 3,500 yards	Postrun ride: easy	Long morning run: 20 miles	

several minutes in length, or a time trial, or some other kind of fast session, mostly on the flat. From noon to 1:30 P.M., I swim in the masters' program, 4,800–5,000 yards. I eat during the 15-minute drive between the pool and my office. I also eat a little on the way home before I run at 5:30. Since I run long and hard on Sundays, I usually run an easy 6 to 7½ miles on Mondays. I follow the run with 30–40 minutes of weightlifting. Then I sit in the hot tub for about 15 minutes. Because Virginia works really hard, too, I sometimes make dinner. There are times when we're both so tired that we go out and eat fast food—I don't want to sit in a restaurant and wait for the waiter. That's a typical Monday.

Dave Epperson

At the starting line.

I bike, swim, and run every day, but I lift weights in my garage only on Mondays, Wednesdays, and Fridays. I tried to research weightlifting and asked other people what kind of program would be best for a triathlete, but no one seemed to know. Finally, I created my own program, which combines a lot of different blocks, pulleys, and weights.

The only time my program changes drastically is before a race. I usually taper off five or six days beforehand by reducing my mileage and improving the quality of my workouts. I stretch a lot, get plenty of rest, and maybe have a massage. Also, I try to go to the race location three or four days early to avoid the distractions of home and settle myself before the event.

Returning from a race, I have to ensure that I recuperate and don't overtrain. Sometimes it can be hard to discriminate between laziness and a genuinely overtrained condition. I have to listen carefully to my body's signals. If I am overtrained, I back off for a day and reduce my mileage. It would probably be better not to do anything at all, but my guilt feelings won't let me. I'm also addicted to the endorphins I get from running; I don't get them as much from biking or swimming. If I miss even one run, I have all kinds of problems; I can't cope as well, and I'm tense in the evening.

I train about half the time with my friends and half the time by myself. That works well for me. I like to go out by myself when I'm not sure exactly how I'm going to feel and I don't want to adapt my training program to somebody else's. But always training by yourself can be unhealthy. I don't see how any person can do it on a long-term basis and succeed without becoming a machine. Even Dave Scott, who comes close to being a machine, admits he's ready to train with other people now. He won the Ironman in 1983, however, principally because he became mentally tough by training so relentlessly—all by himself.

It's hard for people at our level to find other athletes to work out with. The top male triathletes aren't available every day, but I do a lot of workouts with Tom Lux and Kevin McCary, top San Diego runners who were coaches for Team J. David. Gary Peterson runs, and I used to run a great deal with Scott Molina.

I train on fuels from a modified Pritikin diet, and I don't eat sugar or snacks. I was an all-American junk food addict for years, and it wasn't until I had a glucose reaction when I was a stoned 16-year-old that I really began to change my attitude to food. I found out I had hypoglycemia. It's probably taken me 12 years to reverse all the bad food habits I had for so long. I usually eat cereal for breakfast and a lot of fruit and grains—maybe too much—during the day.

My short-term training goals are to reverse my second- and third-place finishes. I have had about 18 second-place finishes in the past four years. I want to turn several notions around, such as that Scott Molina can't be beaten in the short events and that when Mark Allen puts his mind to it he's *totally* unbeatable. My long-term training goal is to work to get gradually stronger and faster. This means I don't peak for the big races. While I may be sacrificing the chance of winning now, I will be stronger than other triathletes in five years' time. I want a base as wide as a room so that, years from now, I can still compete in 18–20 races a year. I want to maintain a balance in my life. I'd like to complete my master's degree. To be able to keep everything in balance, be successful in most things you do and very successful in one is extremely difficult—but I want to do it. If a person does everything only marginally, what has he or she accomplished? Nothing.

One of my strongest attributes is my positive attitude, but I

Dave Epperson

*A constant 33-minute
10k split at BUSTS
distance triathlon.*

certainly wasn't born with it. When you've hit rock bottom and you've been afraid and in a lot of bad situations, you appreciate what is good about life. Most people know this, but not very many practice it.

There's a real art to being an optimist. If you are optimistic enough, you can infect others with it. An optimist never sees anyone or anything as entirely bad. Instead, an optimist says, "Here's someone who has a problem. How can I maximize his potential or bring out whatever good he has in him?" An optimist sees *every* problem as solvable.

I think that's why I never quit. I know that my optimistic personality has helped my athletic career as much as my athletic skills have. Because I've been in lots of situations in which I've had to cut it on my own, I've learned to make the right contacts and to enjoy making them; this is crucial. You can't talk to people just because it's good for your career—that always shows through. You must personally care for and be interested in others and in what they do. Sincere caring always comes across, which gives everyone involved a wholesome feeling and benefits everyone.

As to what motivates me, I can't say I've had many earthshaking experiences. I never woke up one morning and said, "I'm going to be a great triathlete," or "I want to be number one." I'm a firm believer in Maslow's theory of self-actualization. I enjoy taking my basic gifts and attempting to combine and maximize them to create a rich and challenging lifestyle. But it has been a gradual process. I was aware early on that I had the basic potential and the brains to utilize it. Some people have the basics but don't know what to do with them. They overtrain or undertrain; they are overconfident or not quite confident enough. You need the tenacity and perseverance to work toward what is actually a far-off goal.

My optimism is most critical during a race. I believe I lost the 1983 Ironman psychologically. In the end, it was a mental race, and Dave Scott was tougher. But it's practice—it's all practice. We really can change our attitudes, but we have to be open to it; we can't wall ourselves in. When Dave passed me in that race, I was depressed, yet I told myself I'd just let him glide a little bit and then reel him back in. I tried to do that—and that's what's important. Even though I came in second, I never allowed myself to be psychologically destroyed by Dave's performance—I relied on and believed in my own possibilities, regardless of how well he was doing. I'm optimistic about the future.

3
MECHANISM 1
BURNING DESIRE

The second half of the 20th century has often been called "the age of leisure" because of the wealth and free time a flourishing industrial society has provided for the Western world. We often assume that any successful member of our culture is motivated by the desire for money or power, that is, for material gain. However, for Scott Molina, a USTS champion, the motivation comes from a very different source.

Molina moved with his wife and child from his small, trailer house in the San Francisco Bay area to the San Diego stable of Team J. David (formerly the best racing team in the sport). He won prize money and bonuses, and from a sponsor's monthly stipend he bought a better car, a condominium, and other materialistic trappings of success. Yet Scott insists that individual excellence is far more important to him than personal possessions. The pure pleasure that comes from performing at his best is like "a juice" that feeds his desire to improve himself constantly. Scott would strive to excel even without money and recognition. For him, the sense of self-esteem that results from doing his best is reward enough.

We all have the potential to be motivated, but some people feed their potential more effectively than others. Webster's dictionary defines *motive* as follows: "**motive,** *n.* some inner drive, impulse, intention, etc., that causes a person to do something or act in a certain way; incentive; goal."

Motives are nurtured impulses that prompt us to act. They are within all of us, yet a popular misunderstanding of motivation is the notion that *desire* can be pumped in from an external source. Some coaches try to pump motivation into their athletes through the use of material incentives, school rallies, cheering spectators, sermons, and pep talks. These methods may raise the anxiety level of a specific athletic performance, but they will truly motivate only if the athlete turns on the switch; they only work if the athletes want them to. Burning desire is a personal, inner flame.

The importance and personal, emotional nature of burning desire can be felt at the starting line of any triathlon. As the last-minute announcements are broadcast and the paddleboarders take their positions in the water, you wait, realizing that scores of fellow triathletes are as well trained as yourself. They are probably equally talented and genetically endowed to win. But only one woman and one man will break the tape first: That triathlete will be the person who has not only arduously trained but also has the burning desire to win.

Standing at the starting line, you may also see or hear triathletes who will surely fail, even though they might be physically capable of winning. Losers imprison themselves within negative thoughts such as "I have to," "I'm tired," "I am overtrained," and "I wish." The star triathlete, on the other hand, is poised, ready to spring, saying "I want to," or "I can," or "I will."

Two of the most essential psychological motivations we all share are fear and desire. Though they are equally powerful, they can take us in opposite directions.

Fear is a negative source of energy; it can cause us to fail by turning our focus backward, replaying disappointments from the past. Desire looks toward the future; it stimulates our motivation as we imagine races won and goals achieved. It is the perfect mental antidote for fear. That which you fear, you become; that which you desire, you can attain. Focusing on the positive will direct you to the realization of your dreams. Desire is the fuel that sparks success; when you can feel the "burn," you have the energy to win.

Desire can be expressed (by Mark Suprenant in this photo) at a finish line by joy.

SCOTT PHILIP MOLINA

Hometown:	Del Mar, California
Date of birth:	February 29, 1960
Height:	6'0"
Weight:	150–155 pounds
Maximum VO$_2$:	73 ml/kg/min
Body fat:	7 percent
Current profession:	Professional triathlete
Athletic achievements:	1982: Sierra Nevada, first place Ironman, fourth place USTS Los Angeles, San Francisco, first place
	1983: Ricoh Ironman, first place Horny Toads Triathlon, first place USTS San Diego, Los Angeles, San Francisco, U.S.T.S. Championships, first place
	1984: World's Toughest Triathlon, first place Kauai Triathlon, first place USTS—Eight first place finishes including championship Big Island Triathlon, first place Wildflower Look Triathlon, first place Twenty-two triathlons in 1984—eighteen first-place finishes.

Bud Light USTS

A young Scott Molina winning his first USTS in 1982.

Dave Epperson

A TRIATHLON JUNKIE

I was born in Pittsburg, California, and lived there for 21 years, one of seven children. Both my parents are very family-oriented. My mom is a small-town girl from Oklahoma. Her own family background wasn't so happy, so as we grew up she always emphasized the importance of family life. My dad came from a strong Mexican-Catholic family, and even now his brothers and sisters all live very close to each other. We're still close. I was number three in a family of seven. My mom drives a school bus, and my father has worked for Dow Chemical for nearly 30 years.

I went to parochial schools for a few years. My mom and dad thought I would get a better education at a school where there wasn't so much violence. I went to Christian Brothers High School, all boys. My parents wanted me to go on to college and get involved in sports programs, so they thought a small Catholic school would make it easier. My dad has been a track fan all his life, so he encouraged me to get into track. In high school, I ran track and cross-country for four years. I also swam for two years, but I found mixing track with swimming very difficult. Each coach wanted me to concentrate on different things, so I would miss the track meets because I had to go swimming and vice versa. I decided to concentrate on running.

My high school career was fairly normal. I was never involved in any trouble or any particularly traumatic experience. I didn't date very much at school although I met my wife, Stephanie, at that time. We didn't start going out until the end of my first year at Los Medanos College. In my second year, I went to the state track meet in the 10,000 meters, ran 31:11, and took seventh. Although I was happy with that, I felt I could have done better. Because I felt I was able to run in the 30-minute range, I really started training hard. In my free time, I'd go into the library and dig up old editions of *Runner's World* or *Track and Field News* just to see how people used to train.

About that time I got involved in the physiology of running and began to think about going to the University of California at Berkeley to study exercise physiology. After I married in 1980, though, I started training for triathlons, and as I got more motivated for the three-sport event, I seemed to lose it for other things. I became a triathlon junkie. I had been getting As and Bs in school, and I had only 1½ years to go before I got my B.A., but I began to lose my concentration.

Finally, I decided I would just train and work for a while, because we didn't have much money. Jenny, our daughter, was born about a year into our marriage, in July 1981, and that put more pressure on me to earn money. I worked some terrible jobs. I was getting $4 an hour and had to work a lot of hours, so I was either working or training and rarely got to spend time with Stephanie or Jenny. It was a difficult time, and I wasn't very happy.

I talked to J. David after I came in fourth in the 1983 Ironman, although it wasn't until I met them again in Nice that they asked me to join the team. We moved to San Diego where I could be closer to the team and my training partners and better weather conditions.

The USTS race in Los Angeles (1982) was a real turning point for me. It was a really competitive race, well recognized, and the first big triathlon event I had won. Earlier, in 1980, I had won a 50-mile

Dave Epperson

Scott and Jenny share a stationary moment.

race, the Feather River 50. I had trained really hard for it. It was raining heavily and many people dropped out—I didn't. My time was 5 hours, 54 minutes. I was very happy about that race.

My greatest nonathletic experience was learning two years ago that I could be a good father (when Jenny was about a year old). I hadn't thought about it before. I started educating myself a little bit by reading books and talking to professional people and learning exactly what I should and should not be doing. Having a child helped me face my adulthood.

I think the burning probably comes from inside somewhere, but I don't know exactly where. I work harder at my training than most people—there *is* a certain urgency. I even write down in my log, "Be patient because you're going to accomplish things." I look at the history of endurance sports, and logically I know that no one can really develop his potential in a year or two. It takes a long time to make the physiological changes in the cardiovascular system, in the capillary vessels, and in the muscles. So I reason with myself that I'm not going to see results right away, at least not the kind of results I really want. But all the same, the sense of urgency never really goes away. In fact, I'm probably compulsive, even though I try not to be.

Two of my younger brothers, Philip and Sean, have a lot more athletic potential than I do, but I don't think they have my drive. I often tell myself that my only limitation is my genes and that no person will be better than me in a triathlon by training harder or smarter than I have. No, the man who beats me will do so only because he had a VO_2 max of 80 by the time he was 10 years old.

Although I'm in touch with my emotions, my drive seems to keep depression and doubt at bay. I usually analyze mistakes I've made and try to learn from them rather than falling into doubts about my potential. A lot of people think about bad things, but I'm usually optimistic and try to think positively. I don't fear injuries, overtraining, or boredom, but I do fear accidents. I think it's inevitable to fear the accidental when you want something so badly and do everything you can to achieve it. Then it's only the accidental that can stop you.

I don't really see myself as a media celebrity in the future. I would rather be like Bjorn Borg, who just concentrated on performing in events and didn't really get too involved in the media or political aspects of the sport—at least not when he was competing. I don't intend to cop out, but I do need an undisturbed training environment, and at present I have an ideal one that I really enjoy. Actually, I'm getting spoiled; sponsorship money does make a difference. It obviously makes it easier for me to focus and to put 100-percent effort into training, but I would still train without it. It would be harder, but I wouldn't lose my drive.

MOLINA'S TRAINING: PROGRESSING PATIENTLY DESPITE THE "FEVER"

I take a fairly scientific approach to training in that I plan my training programs in a careful and fairly detailed manner. I use a yearly program divided into the seasons, though spring is actually a winter/spring because of the way the triathlon year is set up. Races don't really get going until June or July, and the big events are in August, September, and October. Because a triathlon is such an endurance event, our base period should be a little longer than in other sports, so I usually use from January to June as my base months. But my training varies little throughout the year. If I'm preparing for a particular race, I might intensify my training for a two-week period. I write out a very specific set of workouts for two weeks. As I go from day to day, I know just what I'm supposed to do.

I have found that long, easy workouts are a lot better for me than

Dave Epperson

Equally talented in all three sports.

hard, short, fast ones. For example, I haven't run quarter intervals for a few months because I don't like doing them that much. I do a few quarters in August and September, though, just to sharpen up during racing season. When I do long, easy road miles, I seem to recover on a day-to-day basis very quickly even though I'm putting in a lot of hours. I rarely do double swims or bike rides in one day except on the odd occasion when I intended to take a long ride but had to do something else in the afternoon. Overall, I really try to keep to a schedule so that people know when I'm at home and so Stephanie can rely on me to be there at certain hours.

Also, I would recommend weight training to those triathletes who

SCOTT MOLINA'S TRAINING SCHEDULE

YEARLY PATTERN

WINTER/SPRING
Emphasis on technique and endurance
Cycling: positioning and leg movement; climb mountains
Flexibility and preventive maintenance (crucial)
Alternate weeks: emphasis on running/emphasis on cycling

SUMMER
Keep weight down. Watch it. Stick to schedule. One-day taper. Add motor pacing. Take advantage of the heat; use it.

LATE SUMMER AND FALL: RACING SEASON
Add more motor pacing. Decrease weight training. Harder running but fewer hills. Cut *back* for the big ones. Let the previous work come through.

WEEKLY PATTERN (WINTER/SPRING)

SUNDAY
AM: Long run, fun, in hills; optional easy 2 hours on bike
PM: Run 6–7 with 8–10 fast 200s near end; swim easy 3,500m

MONDAY
AM: Run steady hour, Easy 3–4 hours on bike.
PM: Swim 3,000–4,000 yards and lift weights.

TUESDAY
AM: 1 hour steady with fartlek run. Three hours riding.
PM: Swim 4,000 yards.

WEDNESDAY
AM: Steady hour run. Long, easy ride, 6–7 hours
PM: Swim 4,000m (not too hard!)
Shorter weight workout (heavy!)

EVERY DAY
Stretching, back work, daily nap

THURSDAY
AM: Ride steady 3–4 hours in hills
PM: Swim 4,000m shorter repeats, pullouts
Hard run workout, 6–8 miles (timed)

FRIDAY
AM: Ride steady 3–4 hours (50+ miles) flat
PM: Weights followed by good 5,000+ meters in water (timed)

SATURDAY
Steady hour run or road race
Long hard ride with team/group, 3+ hours
Swim 4,000–5,000m pullouts

SCOTT MOLINA'S TRAINING DIARY
MARCH 11–17

SUNDAY, MARCH 11
Took Jenny to McDonald's for breakfast. Then ran a steady 2:10 out San Dequito Road, round Rancho, next to Lagoon to end of Solana Beach and back. A good, sunny, nice 18. Lifted really well at Lomas followed by a straight DPS 2,800 m. Napped. Ran a really good hour up to T.P., down trails to beach, back up, and home up D.M. Heights Road. Really punching it on hills. Knee creaky. A solid 8.5.

MONDAY, MARCH 12
Rode a steady-med. 4 hours on Powgy, San Pasqual, Escondido, broken for donuts. About 65 miles. Legs not too bad. Ate, napped. Swam a steady DPS 4,000m at Lomas with 35 pullouts. Then broken (pit stops!) but steady 6 miles on coast. 50 sit-ups, leg raises.

TUESDAY, MARCH 13
Ran a hard 10 on flats. 6–7 A.M., on San Dequito Road and sawdust trail. Really hurt. Humid. Sweaty! Home for a break. Stretch. Rode medium 50m Bernardo-Scripps loop. Sunny, warm, good winds. Felt good. Ran a good, solid 55 minutes on Rancho Trails—lots of hard, long hills. About 8.5.

WEDNESDAY, MARCH 14
Rode long with Ron. Out and back on coast and loop of Mission Viejo. Some rain, lots of good tailwinds. A solid 7 hours. 135 miles. Lifted really hard at Lomas. 50 sit-ups. Swam steady 2,800m.

THURSDAY, MARCH 15
Rode an easy 3½ hours, about 50. Sunny, warm. Wore tights. Mostly flat. Ran a steady 55 minutes. About 7.5. Some hills. Swam a steady DPS 4,200m. Straight. Arms tired from yesterday.

FRIDAY, MARCH 16
Rode 3 hours, 35 miles or so. San Pasqual Loop with Gary and Decker, Fast, too. 65. Ran a pretty hard, very sweaty (warm, sunny) 1¼ hours from pool. Lots of good hills. About 12. Swam 1,500 and went home. Pooped.

SATURDAY, MARCH 17
Ran a whole 5 miles on T.P. reserve trails. Some good running, though. Sunny, nice. Business and family day. Ate. Relaxed. Not a bad week, though. 50 sit-ups.

MARCH 11–17
TOTAL TRAINING DISTANCE (MILES)

	BIKE	RUN	SWIM
Sunday	0	26.5	1.8
Monday	65	6	2.5
Tuesday	50	18.5	0
Wednesday	135	1.0	1.8
Thursday	50	7.5	2.6
Friday	65	12	1.0
Saturday	0	5	0
TOTALS	365mi	75.5mi	7.7

Dave Epperson

Scott Molina: *Preparing for the Las Vegas Triathlon.*

SCOTT MOLINA'S TRAINING DIARY
MARCH 18–24

SUNDAY, MARCH 18
Rode to Long Beach and back with Ron.. Flat city. Good winds. Sunny, warm, great day. Felt good. Very steady. 9+ hours, about 170 miles. Done at 3:30. At 6:20 lifted OK at Lomas. Then a hardy, nonstop 2,800m, 25 pullouts, 75 sit-ups.

MONDAY, MARCH 19
Ran a relaxed (felt loose and fast) but fast 70-minute A.M. on Carmel Valley Trails. Warm 70-degree morning, sunny. A good 11. Rode a pretty fast 2¾ hours on Scripps Hill–Kearny Villa Genessee ride. Sunny 80 degrees, really nice. Felt good so swam a mostly paddles 3,000m at Lomas, then some "swim-bench" in weight room. 75 sit-ups.

Scott Molina is noted for his high-mileage training weeks.

TUESDAY, MARCH 20
At 8:15 ran a fast 1 2/3 hours on Carmel Valley Trails. Nice, no shirt, 80 degrees. 6-minute pace, about 16 miles. Felt great. Rode a hot, breezy 2:45 on Del Dios, San Marcos loop. Some good hills. Legs OK. No late P.M. workouts.

WEDNESDAY, MARCH 21
Rode to Mission Bay to meet Mark and Jody. Rode to Tecate and back (95) from the bay. Lots of long, hard hot (85 degrees) hills. Really worked. 110 total. 6:10 on bike. Lifted extremely hard and thorough at Lomas. Just like the old days. 100 sit-ups (incline). Pumped. Then a hard, straight 3,200m, fast.

THURSDAY, MARCH 22
Ran a pretty fast, peppy 55 minute A.M. on Del M. beach run. Sunny, warm, great! Then rode Friars-Mission Gorge—67 loop with Gary. A stop at Zonas. Hard on hills. A good 65. Sunny, windy, but nice. Napped 1½. Swam a hard 4,000m at Lomas. Intervals. Then ran a hard 8 on coast with Gary (out). Sore, tired.

FRIDAY, MARCH 23
Rode 6+ hours with Gary to Rainbow, Fallbrook & Hills to and fro up to 85 degrees. Really nice out. Worked hard. Legs beat. Napped 1½ hours. Late to Lomas. Lifted extremely hard again (minus deltoids). Getting it back. 100 sit-ups. Then a pretty hard, continuous 2,500m in water.

SATURDAY, MARCH 24
Ran a very solid two hours (6–8 A.M.) on Sorrento Penasq. Cany. Mx trails. T.P.H.S.—home. Good hills. Clear, calm, cool morning. Felt good. Tired at end. 50 sit-ups. Rode San Clemente with group. Jammed 7½ on freeway going out. Nice day, 85! Legs OK. Head tired. Napped 1½. Woke up pooped! Swam pretty fast, hard 3,200 straight at Lomas. Pooped. What a week. Cycling coming on strong!

MARCH 18–24
TOTAL TRAINING DISTANCES (MILES)

	BIKE	RUN	SWIM
Sunday	150	0	2.0
Monday	50	7	2.0
Tuesday	50	8	2.2
Wednesday	135	3	4.0
Thursday	45	16	4.0
Friday	115	0	0
Saturday	65	5	2.5
TOTALS	610mi	39mi	16.7mi

have the time. I used to use weights a lot in high school but stopped until last year. Now I lift for an hour, three days a week, to build my strength. I use heavy weights for sets of about six or seven repetitions. I've noticed my times in the pool are definitely improving, and I feel stronger.

I don't eat an enormous amount of sugar, but probably more than is good for me. I drink lots of water. I eat two dinners, one before swimming and again in the evening, when I eat leftovers. I make vegetables, chicken, fish, and, once in a while, spaghetti.

As to training with or without others, I prefer not to drain myself mentally by continually pushing myself alone. I do train alone about half the time, but I'm confident that I can push myself in a race without having to do it every day. My body receives the same training effect whether it's pushed by me or others, but it takes the pressure off when I let others do it for me now and then. Usually, I train with Mark Allen, Gary Peterson, George Hoover, Chris Miller, and the Tinleys (mostly Scott). We compete against each other, but it's not competition in the cutthroat sense. We agree to help each other work hard and improve. However, when we get to a race, we shake hands, say, "Good luck, hope you do well," and then we're on our own. We have a love for each other that comes from sharing similar athletic backgrounds and because all of us found this sport relatively late in our careers. We're all trying to reach our potential, so we understand what each other is going through. I like the closeness we have; it feels good. We share parts of ourselves, but we don't use them against each other. We talk about caring for each other: "Thanks for the workout, Gary; here's a six-pack of beer. Thanks." This kind of communication is important. I feel I am an introvert, but I also think most of the other people I train with are introverts. I deeply appreciate the help my friends give me.

In addition to all my other training techniques and methods, I do a lot of things to prevent injuries and that allows me to train day after day. I stretch a great deal, I take a lot of Jacuzzis and massages, and I always try to get a good night's sleep. I also take naps these days because I'm no longer working two jobs or going to school. I also try to keep my days free of distractions. All this is as important as my training.

I would like to impress upon all young triathletes that no one gets to the top in a flash. We all have to be patient with our progress. You must look at your long-term development and ask yourself, "How will the training I'm doing now help me prepare for next year's training?" Be reasonable in your expectations. It seems to me that many people get the "fever" and improve but soon get burned out. The triathlon should enhance your lifestyle, not become it.

4

TOOL 2

LIMITLESS IMAGINATION

At one time I was absolutely convinced that I couldn't write. Throughout high school, I was a B-minus English student; I scored poorly on the SAT college entrance exams in English, but my math scores saved the day. I took the UC Berkeley entrance exam in English, and one more time I bombed. Forced to take "bonehead English," I passed only because one of the questions on the final exam was: "Write about anything you want." In anticipation, I had memorized a *Time* magazine article entitled "Federal Aid to Education." I passed. English/A and B were a struggle ending with a low C average. The school system had convinced me that I couldn't write.

Then, one evening after I had lectured to an audience about one of my favorite topics—the second-class citizenship of the female athlete—a listener challenged me to put my spoken words into action and write a book. I automatically responded, "I can't write." After years of negative reinforcement, my inner automaton was programmed to reject the challenge. It was programmed with the limited image of myself as a handicapped, illiterate writer.

Later that day I nagged myself with a stream of self-talk. "Sally, why don't you write about these issues?" I chided myself. "Why not create societal change through the written word?" I had no suitable excuse; that day I decided I would write a book.

I had never written a magazine article, a poem, *anything*, yet I knew that I could write a book. For my subject, I chose my new love—the sport of triathlons. I thought of the book as an experiment to see if what I had to say would be interesting to others.

My first roadblock was negativity—my friends' as well as my own. My associates knew how long it takes to write a book and the lack of available information about triathlons at that time. "What is there to write about?" one person asked. The skepticism merely heightened the challenge. I armed myself with allies and assets—a close friend could type 100-plus words a minute and had access to a word processor, and another knew an editor. I made the time available by getting up at 4:00 A.M. and writing until daylight—every day—until the book was complete.

To our wildest dreams, we must attach a reality. For the writer, reality is a publisher. Who would publish a book such as this? I sent letters to targeted specialty publishers, and they responded with rejections. They had never heard of triathlons, nor did they think the sport was "the coming of a new fitness boom of the '80s." Compounding my difficulties with the publishers was the fact that I had no writing credentials—it was a risky bet at best. Not to be defeated, I reached into the deepest reserves of my incurable optimism—and my checking account—and resorted to what writers euphemistically refer to as "vanity press." I published the book myself. It was typewriter-printed, featuring six photographs and a front jacket with strong, Grecian-type graphics. I stored cases of *Triathlon: A Triple Fitness Sport* in my garage. The marketing plan was threefold: I peddled them at races, placed small mail-order advertisements in publications I could afford, and sent complimentary copies with press releases. I sold 8,000 copies in six months, and four different publishers came knocking at my door. The publisher I chose produced a beautifully typeset book with 90 photos and a full-color cover; within a year we had sold 50,000 copies, outselling any running book on the market.

The book serves as an example of how someone with a preprogrammed inferiority complex can be changed. It required limitless imagination, working along with the other tools and mechanisms, for the dream to become a reality, but it worked for me and will work for you. Limitless imagination is not something you are born with; it is something that you can develop from within. Each of us has a life-governing subconscious device, a programmable automaton. The automaton serves a critical role in changing our wildest dreams into reality, because it houses our self-image. It is a data bank from which we make all our conscious decisions.

The automaton cannot distinguish between input that is real and input that is imaginary. Like a ballistic missile system, the automaton is a highly sophisticated electronic network that unerringly seeks the target through the use of input and output feedback. To

Sally Edwards lectures on one of her favorite topics.

prove that Chicken Little was wrong, dream your wildest dreams, feed your automaton that visualization, and the input program will interpret the incoming message as real. Your visualization will also become real.

Let's say you are having trouble staying on a training program. You decide that you are going to run at 5:30 every morning. You go to the automaton and tell it that you will train every morning at 5:30. It wants to believe you but has heard the line before and knows that your dedication is too hit and miss and that you usually feel guilty when you miss. The automaton goes to its memory bank and brings up your file, which reads: difficulty in maintaining a program of exercise, frequent lapses in training, feelings of resultant disappointment. The automaton next checks your self-image file and reads that you see yourself as a nonathlete, that you think of yourself as slow, a weakling, a klutz. The automaton can only conclude that you are, in fact, a nonathlete who is likely to continue on a pattern of fitness irregularity.

If you want to change, you must allow your limitless imagination to develop by removing the blinders that prevent you from seeing all of the possibilities that invite opportunity. Children know this. They play a game called "Let's Pretend." They fantasize about being cowgirls, Martians, or Indiana Jones. For them, Halloween is a real world. Adults can play the game of life by seeing themselves breaking the finish tape, picking up the trophy at the awards ceremony, putting on the finisher's T-shirt over an exhausted and salt-sweaty body. Successful athletes know that an improved self-image reprograms the automaton into validating that they can go farther, faster, and stronger than they are going now and that there are no limits on how good they can become. Limitless imagination is a tool that can reveal to you all the possibilities of self-change—if you want to use it.

JOHN KENNEDY HOWARD

Hometown: Encinitas, California

Date of birth: August 16, 1947

Height: 6'1"

Weight: 160 pounds

Maximum VO$_2$: 82 ml/kg/min

Body fat: 5–9 percent

Current profession: Professional athlete, owner of Multi-fitness, a company that supplies his signature model bicycle to athletes

Athletic achievements:

1968, 1972, 1976 United States Olympic Cycling Team—Time Trial and Road Race, National Time Trial, Road Race & Cycle Cross National Champion

1971: Pan American Games Cycling Road Racing, gold medal

1981: Ironman Champion

1984: Tri-Fed USA National Long Course Championship (Denver Mile High), age division winner, second overall.

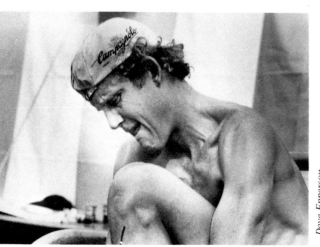

Dave Epperson

John Howard: 1981 Ironman run transition.

Dave Epperson

FROM OLYMPIC CYCLIST TO TRIATHLETE

I grew up in Springfield, Missouri, in the Ozark Mountains. My father worked for the government as a medical technician. He probably had more of a mental influence on me than my mother did, although I probably acquired more physical endurance from her side of the family.

My younger brother lives in Austin, Texas. He has an auto repair business and fixes exotic sports cars. We both have a thing about

Willy McCleary

Cycling to a world record of 514 miles at the "Pepsi 24 Hour Marathon."

fast cars; that's all we seemed to care about as kids. Back then, my real interests lay in motorcycling and go-cart racing. We even had a racing sailboat and were part of the Rhodes Bantam fleet on the Missouri lakes. I suppose racing is in my blood. I went from cars to motorcycles, and eventually to bicycles. Bicycling was a radical change for me, but I became fond of the physical exertion and began discovering my potential for endurance sports.

I had played some football in my early years, mainly because my father had been a football player during his college years, and he wanted me to do the same thing. When I quit football, he jokingly threatened to disown me—football meant a lot to him. But at the age of 18, I entered my first bike race anyway.

After that, I went to college for four years, but I never graduated because I was drafted during my senior year. I had been in Mexico

Willy McCleary

An extraordinary cyclist—
John Howard en route to winning 1983 U.C. San Diego criterium.

for several months, racing in the 1968 Olympics, so I lost my college deferment. I managed to hang on to it for a while, but finally they just came and got me. I went into the Army in 1971 and stayed for two years.

At first I was really paranoid. It was right at the height of the Viet Nam crisis, so I was worried about that. Also, I was concerned that I wouldn't be able to ride my bike. I had no guarantees.

I started making phone calls. I talked to my battalion commander and told him that cycling was really what I wanted to do. It turned out that he was a former bike racer from Indiana University; he was very receptive to me. The Army let me out of Advanced Individual Training and allowed me to train full-time. For the next 18 months I was in special services. In fact, we had six service members on the Pan Am team, and we did very well. We won four medals in the Pan Am Games, and that was the best performance record of any of the armed forces athletes that year; consequently, they let us ride our bikes full-time for another year. There was a lot of controversy, though, in 1972 because everyone considered us to be professionals. Things have definitely changed.

After I came out of the Army, I started to go back to college because I had only about 13 hours to complete for a bachelor's degree, but I decided against that because I really couldn't figure out how I would use it. I went to work. First, I was a bicycle sales rep for a Swedish company, so I got to race in Sweden. Then I worked in public relations for Campagnolo, followed by a consulting job with Exxon in which we worked on a composite materials project. We developed a superexotic graphite hybrid bicycle. It was way ahead of its time and was extremely expensive. We sold quite a few. After three years of this, Exxon suddenly pulled out of sporting goods altogether. I returned to Campagnolo for two more years but decided in 1979 that I wasn't really making enough money, so I went off on my own.

HOWARD'S TRAINING: PART EFFORT, PART RECOVERY

The methods I used to win the 1981 Ironman are fairly indicative of the kind of approach I usually take, although, looking back, I have streamlined my program a bit.

I started training for my first triathlon in 1978, and I made a lot of mistakes. I ran my first marathon after only a month of running and ended up with shinsplints. I would definitely not run that distance now without a lot more background in the sport. Coming from a cycling background into running is very tough. It's a lot easier to make a cyclist out of a runner than it is a runner out of a cyclist. If I were starting now, I would concentrate more energy on the sports I am not good in than in the ones I am. I think you need to put your sport of origin on the back burner when you begin training for a triathlon.

In 1981, I tried to do that. I spent more time running and swimming and started doing something I hadn't done since high school track days: speed work. However, the backlog of miles still wasn't there, and I went from shinsplints to stress fractures. I resorted to long, slow distance again.

I kept very accurate logs of my weekly mileage. In swimming, especially, I was doing a great deal of work and doing it properly. I was swimming about 50,000 yards a week, two hours a day. I had a coach and worked out with a masters' group, but I'm not a swimmer by nature, and I had a lot of trouble with technique, especially at first.

I tried to do all three sports in one day, but I think that may have been another mistake. Now I feel it's more important to do quality work and not worry so much about doing all three on the same day. Part of training is recovering, yet so few athletes seem to understand the importance of that. You have to spend some time letting

Dave Epperson

John Howard (far right) awaiting starting gun.

the body find its own level before you train again. I was training for a very important race; I had to take a week off to travel to New York. Throughout the week I said to myself, "I'm losing so much," but my first day back I did a 5½-hour workout, and I felt great. I'm not saying every athlete should take a whole week off, but some time off is a must. I structure my own program to allow for recovery by following a hard week with an easy week and so on, rather than just trying to grind it out every day in exactly the same way. To avoid injuries—which you are definitely prone to when you don't allow your body sufficient time to recover—you have to do as Plato suggested: "Know thyself." At all costs, avoid injury.

My weight training is minimal. I don't have the time or discipline to pump iron on a regular basis. Whenever I do lift, I do high reps with low weight to avoid building bulk. However, I do think that, when you're in a stressful situation, diet is extremely important, although it may not be as crucial in a freewheeling, easygoing kind of lifestyle. If your diet is bad, and you're under a lot of stress at the same time, that's when things really start to crash down on you. I eat a lot of fiber, raw foods, fruits, and vegetables. I also eat a lot of carbohydrates, but I'm not a big protein consumer. I know the theory behind the Pritikin diet, and I follow it to a certain extent but not religiously. If I had to endorse any diet, it would probably be his.

Winning is relative. To me, it once meant crossing the finish line first, but as I've grown older and have less time to train, I have had to readjust my priorities. I've begun to view winning as accomplishing my own performance goals. I don't assign myself a placing; it feels better that way. People who set their goals too high spoil it for themselves because they see themselves as finishing a race in a certain position, and when they don't they can only see themselves as failures. You need to be realistic in your projection of goals. If you overextend yourself by overtraining or try to do something that you're not physically or mentally capable of doing, then you may end up letting that unconscious failure adversely affect other aspects of your life.

I never overextend myself. I'm a professional, and I know my reserves and my strengths, so I have rarely given more than that. I know when I reach the point where there's nothing left. I admire athletes who can press beyond that point, but I'm afraid I'm not one of them. I have only so much, and I just try to give it all. As far as finding that reserve and that internal fortitude that it takes to fall down just when you cross the line, it's not me. I finish spent, but rarely collapse.

Because cycling has always been such an intense mind game for me, rather like a chess game, I tend not to view the triathlon that way. I don't see the same kind of repeated mental strategy at work—the most physically fit athlete wins, whereas in cycling that's not always the case. That's why I enjoy the triathlons so much. They are all raw horsepower with very little stress.

Right now my attitude is positive, but I can think of a number of occasions when I've defeated myself by not being 100-percent positive about the outcome of an event. The best feeling in a race is when you cross that line from being just a participant to absolutely knowing you're going to win. When I took over the lead in the 1981 Ironman, it was definitely the highlight of my athletic career—just the marvelous feeling of *knowing* I could do it. I felt there was no way I could lose, and I kept that optimism throughout the event. In fact, when Molina came so close, I made a conscious effort to look strong, happy, and energetic. Psychologically, that may have had an effect—if only a small one—on him. He saw me as determined, and it probably worked a little to his disadvantage.

Once, in an upcoming race, I first heard about the competition I'd be up against, I was a little psyched out. But one night soon after that, I had a dream that I was riding in the race and felt completely satisfied. I wasn't winning it, but I felt good, so I interpreted that as a victory. Since then I have felt very calm about racing and the kind of competition I'll be facing. I try to pay attention to dreams. Part of my positive attitude may lie in visualizing things optimistically. If you allow yourself to think defeat, you'll probably end up defeating yourself.

I also believe it's important to maintain your composure under fire in an event or in life, which means you have to know how to contain your fears and anxieties. You can't increase your pace in order to compensate for losing time. If you do that when you're already flatout, you'll never finish well. Again, I think you have to know yourself and your own limitations, and if it isn't enough, then

John Howard Triathlon
Weekly Training Schedule
From **8-12-80** to **8-19-80**

	Sleep (Hr.)	Pulse Morn.	Pulse Eve.	Weight Morn.	Weight Eve.	Distance, Mi., Yd. Run	Distance, Mi., Yd. Bike	Distance, Mi., Yd. Swim	Calisthenics Yoga	Calisthenics Wt.	(Mins) Other
Mon.	8	43	44	159	159	14	60	4700	30	30	
Tue.	7½	44	44	159	160	15	65	4,800	30	30	
Wed.	8	43	44	155	159	18	60	5000	45	30	
Thur.	9	46	45	158	158	12	40	4000	20	20	
Fri.	8	42	45	158	160	12	40	3,900	30	35	
Sat.	9	44	43	159	159	3	35	—	30	—	
Sun.	8	41	42	159	159	20	50	5000	30	20	
Tot.	57½					92	390	27,400	3.5 hrs	2.4 hrs	

Technical:

(1) How did it feel? _Stronger than last week. Easy week helped!_

(2) Were you satisfied with each week's performance? _Yes_

(3) What did you like/dislike about the performance? _Good feeling of growing strength / dull pain in right foot increasing._

Races:

Event _Run_ Distance _10 K_ Time _33:10_ Place _4th_ Course _____

Event _Bike_ Distance _25 mi_ Time _58:56_ Place _1st_ Course _____

Event _Swim_ Distance _100 free_ Time _1·11_ Place _____ Course _____

Race Projections (record upcoming events and personal expectations):

10 K run next week. Hope to break 33 minutes.

Misc (Information about weather, personal evaluation of health, etc.):

100° every day. Health very good. Mind, O.K.

John Howard Triathlon
Weekly Training Schedule
From ___2-7-81___ to ___2-13-81___

	Sleep (Hr.)	Pulse Morn.	Pulse Eve.	Weight Morn.	Weight Eve.	Distance, Mi., Yd. Run	Distance, Mi., Yd. Bike	Distance, Mi., Yd. Swim	Calisthenics Yoga	Calisthenics Wt.	(Mins) Other
Mon.	9	38	37	156	156	10	50	6000	30	30	
Tue.	9	37	40	157	157	8	40	4000	30	15	
Wed.	8½	38	37	156	156	6	35	3000	30	—	
Thur.	9	37	38	155	156	5	30	2000	30	—	
Fri.	8	36	38	156	157	2	25	1000	30	15	
Sat.	8	36	37	156	160	1	10	—	30	—	
Sun.	9	37	41	160	161	—	5	—	15	—	
Tot.	60					32	195	16,000	3.15hrs	1 hr	

Technical:

(1) How did it feel? __Peaked!__

(2) Were you satisfied with each week's performance? __Yes__
(3) What did you like/dislike about the performance? __All__
___Systems are on. Everything feels right.___

Races:

Event _____ Distance _____ Time _____ Place _____ Course _____

Event _____ Distance _____ Time _____ Place _____ Course _____

Event _____ Distance _____ Time _____ Place _____ Course _____

Race Projections (record upcoming events and personal expectations):
___Race tomorrow. 2.4 mile swim — 112 mile bike —___
___26.2 mile run.___

Misc (Information about weather, personal evaluation of health, etc.):
___Weather good. Health perfect.___

Dave Epperson

John Howard set the course record at 1984 Ironman
cycling stage 112 miles in 4 hours, 55 minutes.

it isn't enough. You should never let fear be a factor or let it break your master plan. If you do, I think you'll compound the fear.

As I've grown, I've started to cultivate a feeling of well being about sports and competition. I want to help others improve their ability. I've found that my focus has really shifted from going out to compete to being an advisor. I like to be an information source for any athlete who'll listen to what I have to say. It goes beyond coaching. One of the joys of my life is to find an athlete who has raw ability and to help develop that potential.

When I'm excited about a project, as I am now, I can work very hard on very little sleep. At those times, I can't imagine sleeping past 6:00 A.M. I like to get up in the morning and enjoy that enthusiasm. I usually seem to have more of it, though, in the winter, and I think the reason for that is I'm not competing and training hard on a regular basis. So this year, I'll try to pull some of that enthusiasm from the winter into the summer by possibly competing less or training less and, most important of all, by trying to enjoy all the work. I get so locked in on the regular routine of training that I lose sight of the purpose from the beginning, which was to find some fulfillment, and if I'm not enjoying it, then I have to ask myself, "What's the point of all this?"

I juggle all the different factors of my life by relying on competent people to help me. If I'm training seven hours a day, which is often the case, obviously things need to get done, so I delegate responsibility to those people I trust. I'm very fortunate to have people I can communicate with, and I appreciate knowing they're not out there to take advantage of me in any way. It takes a long time to cultivate those kinds of people.

I'm very content with my life right now and don't really want to change it. The only thing I would like is more time to write; I have a lot more to say about my field.

5
MECHANISM 2
BLIND FOCUS

You know that you can if you think you can. That's the attitude I used to prepare for the 1984 Women's Olympic Trials Marathon. I just decided that I could qualify and did.

Qualification standards required a 2:51:16 marathon finish within a period between the 1983 and the 1984 Boston Marathon dates. The mile splits to hit that magic finish time, if run at an even pace, are 6½-minute miles for 26.2 miles.

It was my limitless imagination that led me to the realization that the accomplishment was possible. It was my burning desire to make the trials that helped me train. But it took blind focus to concentrate all of my energy like a laser beam on that dominant thought—to run the fastest marathon of my life.

My previous best had been in 1980, when I won the Sacramento Marathon in 2 hours, 53 minutes. Since that date, I hadn't seriously trained for the marathon for four years. During the intervening years, I had focused on the triathlon and subsequently had developed a tremendous crosstraining baseline.

This was an entirely new training concept. The study of exercise physiology is so inbred with the specificity theoretical model that most practitioners know nothing else. To be a good runner, they assume you *only* run. Likewise, to be a good swimmer or cyclist, you train only in those disciplines. The same scientists argue that crosstraining will lead to disastrous performances in single-sport races.

The training model I would use for the trials had never been tested:

Take a tremendous crosstraining base and top it off with six weeks of sport-specific running speed work.

My personal experience challenged those archaic principles. The thesis of crosstraining is that, by working other muscle and cardio-respiratory systems, the sport-specific system will improve. By supplementing my running with swimming and cycling, I found that I could indeed run stronger and faster.

I blindly focused all of my attention on running for the final six weeks before my qualifying race, virtually abandoning my bike and swimsuit. I knew that I had a tremendous crosstraining base. The *a la mode* would be high-frequency speed training.

Three times a week—Tuesdays, Thursdays, and one weekend day—I ran fast. As the weeks progressed, my repeat miles dropped from over 6 minutes with a half-mile jog in between to running all four-mile repeats under 5:20. Thursdays would be track workouts, intervals, and 10 quarter-mile repeats that dropped from 85 seconds to 73–75 seconds with a half-lap jog in between. On the weekends, I would road race and continue to watch those times drop. My last test was the Oakland Half-Marathon in February, which I finished in 1:21.

As I trained, I focused my mind on the marathon ahead. I knew that I had to train both my body and my mind and that the mental process of blind focus required that I vividly imagine myself running 26.2 at a 6½-minute mile pace. By picturing and feeling in detail the successful outcome, the internal image is changed from one of doubt and uncertainty to one of positive expectancy. By taking my limitless imagination as a tool, I laser-beamed it into such intense focus that I succeeded and qualified for the Olympic Trials

Sally Edwards approaching the finish line of the 1984 Phoenix Marathon in a time of 2:50:57, qualifying her for the Olympic Marathon Trials.

marathon. A lifetime dream came true and I was on the starting line for the first Women's Olympic Trials Marathon, a race that symbolized that women had an equal apportunity to compete in endurance athletics.

SYLVIANE AND PATRICIA PUNTOUS

Hometown:	San Diego, California
Date of birth:	December 28, 1960
Height:	5'6½"
Weight:	122 pounds
Maximum VO$_2$:	68 ml/kg/min on treadmill
Body fat:	9–10 percent
Current profession:	Professional triathletes

Athletic achievements:

1982: USTS Seattle, first place
1983: Bud Light Ironman Championships; Mighty Hamptons Triathlon, first place
Bud Light USTS Series National Championships
1984: Bud Light Ironman Championships; Canadian Olympic Trials Marathon
Mighty Hamptons Triathlon, first place

Dave Epperson

Dave Epperson

Sylviane and Patricia before the start of the 1983 All Women's Triathlon, San Francisco.

Two are better than one,
because they have a good reward for their labor.

Ecclesiastes 4:9

Our parents came to Montreal, Canada, in the early 1950s. We were born in 1960 in Canada. At seven, our mother wanted us to learn how to swim, so she registered us in a local swimming club. She always reminds us how scared we were at first. She says that we were terrified to even put our noses in the water! When we were eight, we began to enter small swimming races. We usually won, so we joined the best club in Montreal, and from the age of nine, we began to train very hard, swimming before and after school every day.

At 12 years old, we were very good. I [Patricia] was better than Sylviane at that point, but after a while I peaked out. I think it was because people told me I would start to have a bad time and that as I changed into a woman I would not be able to continue doing as well. This affected me badly. After that, Sylviane started to do very well, and I dropped behind. Sylviane was ranked 19th in all of Canada while I was ranked about 30th. I would train with Sylviane and be equally good, but during the races I always seemed to fall

Dave Epperson

Patricia Puntous during the 1984 Bud Light Ironman race.

back. Consequently, I stopped competitive swimming at 16, and Sylviane kept going for just a summer more. Both of us realized we would no longer improve in our swimming. We knew we would never make the top 10, so we decided to try something else.

We participated in some track meets at school and did well, so we joined a club. After a year of training we were able to beat some fairly good runners from Quebec. We continued racing for our club for two more years when we began to get restless and rebellious. We would go out a lot to dance and see movies, and our performance began to reflect all of our late nights. We had arguments with our coach and the federation, so we quit for a season. When we came back, we were determined to complete a marathon. We ran our first marathon in 2:48:54 in Ottawa. The federation offered sponsorship to runners who finished under 2:49. We had jokingly

Dave Epperson

1984 USTS/Chicago—Sylviane Puntous.

told our friends we would run the race in 2:48:59, and we actually came close to that. After the marathon we trained with a coach again.

In 1982, I [Patricia] had an injury that was so bad that I had to stop running for three months, but I made it worse than it initially was by trying to run on it too soon. I [Sylviane] continued to run while she was injured, but I didn't really want to, so I didn't do very well. During that period of time we saw the Ironman on television. The idea came into our heads to try a triathlon because we were swimmers and runners anyway, and we had a lot of endurance. We began to swim and bike, and some friends coached us a little. The USTS Seattle race was our first triathlon, and we won. We were surprised that we had done so well; we thought it would be harder than it was. Track seemed much harder in comparison.

After the Seattle race, we returned to running because we wanted to do a good marathon. We moved to Florida for the winter because during that season there are lots of big races with prize money, and a lot of well-known athletes compete there. We entered the Orlando Marathon and did it in 2:42:53, although we felt that we were capable of doing it in under 2:40.

In Florida we met Orlando Valdez, who is now our manager. His father had a big contracting business, and Orlando worked for him. After we moved back to Montreal, we called Orlando every day and talked to him on the phone. At the time, we were unhappy with our lives in Canada, and he was equally unhappy with his life as a general contractor in Florida. We decided to live together in California, and Orlando became our manager. He got us really involved in triathlons.

So we all went to Bass Lake, and people sponsored us and gave us a chalet for the summer while we trained. We were very lucky. After the USTS Championship, we tried for the Canadian Olympic Trials in the marathon, but we did not do well. We did it because our family, coach, and friends wanted us to. That's probably why we did so badly. How can you do well in something if you don't even want to do it? After the trials we moved to San Diego, where we live now. Up to this year, we've basically had to live off the money we've won from races, but now we have a big sponsorship contract, so we aren't under such pressure to race for money.

Both our parents work. Our mother is a waitress, and our father works for the Quebec highway department. Two years ago, we completed our BAs in physical education in Montreal, through the University of Quebec, but we've never even tried to pursue careers as teachers. No one in our family is athletic; we were lucky that we were exposed to athletics at school and found our potential early. We never really had any problem as females in sport except when we first began running on the street. Running wasn't such a popular sport then, so we used to get a lot of whistles and catcalls from men. Apart from that, however, our family and friends seemed very proud of our success in sport and have never tried to dissuade us from participating.

When we want something very badly, we simply go for it. We are determined, focused, disciplined people. Both of us are fairly shy, and, because we always have each other, we don't feel like we have to go out much. Consequently, we're not very sociable. We don't like to be around too many people; for example, we don't enjoy going out to eat with lots of people because we don't like to feel we have to say something when we don't want to. Most of our friends are triathletes, although we're not exceptionally close to them. In Montreal we have friends, but because we have each other, we tend to forget them once we move away.

Noel Black

Sylviane (right) and Patricia Puntous finished first and second at the 1983 Bud Light Ironman Triathlon World Championship in Hawaii. The twins from Montreal, Canada, both shattered the previous women's record of 10:54:08 set in 1982.

Also, we're fairly impatient, and that's why we didn't want to pursue our careers in physical education. We'd have no patience with the kids. Neither of us really thinks about marriage and having a family; it just isn't a concern for us right now.

We are different from each other to a small degree, although not overly so. Sylviane is more aggressive in races than I [Patricia] am, but I am more aggressive during our training, so we balance each other out. We tend to think the same way and have the same tastes, especially in clothes. If we buy identical garments, we try to buy them in different colors. We have the same size feet, so often we don't know whose shoes belong to whom. Sometimes we communicate nonverbally, which can be useful when we're in a big group of people and can't express something out loud. We understand each other.

It's really important to us to win, and you can win only by focusing on the pain. Our competitive experience in track and field and in the marathon has given us the ability to withstand a lot of pain; we try to regard it as a challenge. When we race, we try not to doubt our abilities. We tell ourselves no one is tougher than we are and no one can tolerate as much pain as we can. We always try to outlast everyone else. We concentrate on the race completely and try never to slow down. Each time we catch someone we get an extra boost. We think we can do the Ironman faster, although in 1983 we didn't feel as if we were racing it so much as surviving it. But at least in a race as long as the Ironman you can stop and walk

Herb Nelson

Sylvianne and Patricia at the 1984 USTS/Chicago Triathlon.

now and then without losing your position; in a short race you can never let up.

We know we can get faster and stronger because we feel as if we are only beginning. It takes many years of experience and training to really reach your potential—especially in something like the triathlon. We want to try new sports as well. We were good at running when we lived in Canada; then we decided that wasn't enough, so we tried triathlon and proved we could do that, too. Now we are thinking of attempting another sport, something very different. Once we have reached our goal, we need another challenge.

PUNTOUS TRAINING: IN TWOS

We swim at noon four days a week with the master's program at University of California-San Diego. On the fifth day, we go to the La Jolla Cove for the afternoon and swim by ourselves. Every week we set a goal: 300 miles on the bike, 60–75 miles of running, and 20,000 yards of swimming. Within each week we usually do a long bike ride, a long run, some interval workouts in our running, a hard run, a 50-mile time trial, and also some hill work on the bike. When we swim, we always do intervals, although some days are tougher than others. For example, we may do repeats at 500 one day, but the next day they'll probably be shorter. On Saturdays, we try to go on a long

PUNTOUS TWINS' MID-SEASON TRAINING REGIMEN

DAY	TIME		NOTES
MONDAY	A.M.	Easy 25+ bike	1. Average 4–6½ hours a day of training
	noon	Pool swim—intervals 5,000 yards	
	P.M.	Run intervals	
TUESDAY	A.M.	50-mile bike time trial	2. Distance goals: swim 20,000 yards
	noon	Pool swim—intervals 5,000 yards	bike 300 miles run 60–75 miles
	P.M.	Easy run 6+ miles	
WEDNESDAY	noon	1–3 hours' cycling Pool swim—intervals 5,000 yards A hard, fast run, usually 10 miles Relaxed 5–8-mile run	
THURSDAY	noon	Pool swim—intervals 5,000 yards Hilly bike workout	
FRIDAY	noon	Cycle 1–3 hours Ocean swim— endurance 1–2 miles Run 8–10 miles	
SATURDAY		Long bike, 4–5 hours	
SUNDAY		Long run, 15+ miles	

bike ride, and on Sundays we try to go on a long run. We don't swim on the weekends. We work out four to seven hours a day. We usually go to bed early—9:00 P.M., sometimes 8:00. Now and then we go out to see a movie or to a dance. We also love clothes shopping during the late afternoons, if we have time.

We usually taper off our training a few days before a race, but for a big one like the Ironman, we begin to taper two weeks before; we go 200 miles on the bike rather than 300. Because we need to go easy at this point, when we are tired, we don't work out. For the Ironman you have to be very fit. If not, it's over. All your training has to be complete long before the race. You can't take any chances. In fact, we try to arrive at least two weeks before the race just to get used to the different climate and environment.

In 1983, we were sick about a week before the race. We were tired, nauseous, and had completely lost our appetites. It was probably due to the climate and food as well as prerace nerves. Everyone seemed to expect us to win, but we ourselves never know if we will or not. Racing the Ironman is not as much fun as it used to be; now there is too much pressure. Everyone waits to beat you. That's why we're lucky to have each other. We're stronger that way. A lot of athletes are alone, so they have to fight loneliness, too.

When we don't feel like training, we wake up extra early and try to get everything done by noon. Then we'll go shopping or something else that's fun. If there were no Ironman, we would do half of the training we do now, but even for that you have to be in top condition, and you have to discipline yourself in order to make your mind as tough as your body. Occasionally, we'll train with other people, and it is usually a lot of fun and gives us an extra boost, but really we feel we need to work out with each other most of the time so that we learn to rely on ourselves and not other people. Then we feel tougher for the race.

We try to avoid junk food in our diet. If we do eat a dessert like ice cream, for example, we try not to eat any more sugar for a few days after that. We are vegetarians, so we don't eat meat; and we also try to avoid a lot of fat. We eat plenty of bread, cereal, and rice.

6

TOOL 3

DECISIVE CONTROL

I grew up the American Way; I was the fourth child and only daughter of a Navy aviator and a housewife, J. P. and Gaye Edwards. We moved every year, changing schools, friends, and, for me, Brownie and then Girl Scout troops. When Dad retired as a commander, we settled on four acres in the country. I loved animals and bought a Hereford steer named Bobbie. My brothers tried their hand at sports, but, as it turned out, I was the star athlete of the family, the typical All-American girl. I was cheerleader, songleader, 4-H member, and student-body vice president. Like my three older brothers, I went off to college after I graduated from high school. At UC Berkeley I lived in a sorority house: Kappa Alpha Theta. I played intercollegiate athletics, played student senator politics, and played with a fraternity man, a Delta Upsilon. My story continued down the path that others had determined for me. I stayed in school for a master's degree in physical education–exercise physiology. My master's thesis even predicted my interest in long-distance athletic pursuits: "Effect of Fatiguing Exercise on the Response Latencies of the Director Motor Response, the H Reflex, the Achilles Tendon Reflex, and the Simple Reaction Time." It was about fatigue.

It was easy to let others make the decisions. After graduate school, it was a one-year stint in Viet Nam with the American Red Cross, another year to travel around the world with a backpack and the man from Delta Upsilon. The two of us settled in Sacramento,

Elizabeth Jansen (left) and Sally Edwards (right)—For these two triathletes, business is an opportunity to integrate the love of sports and work.

where I worked as a junior high school teacher for two years, then to Monterey Peninsula College for one more teaching assignment.

I didn't realize until I was 28 that I was in charge of my own life, that I could make life happen rather than let others decide how it would happen to me. I left the teaching job, the love of travel, and the Delta Upsilon fraternity man, and along with Elizabeth Jansen, my best friend from cheerleading days, bought an 1880s Victorian in Sacramento and started an athletic shoe and apparel business: Fleet Feet. We now have 25 franchised stores across the United States. I have never been sorry I took that risk.

We all have to make choices in life; decisive control is about making those choices from the driver's seat. Instead of allowing astrological signs, the federal government, or family and friends to make the decisions, we can determine our own destinies.

It starts with believing in the great natural law of the universe: the law of cause and effect. We—not fate, luck, or even upbringing—determine the cause. Life is a do-it-yourself game. As Voltaire suggested, we, the players, must accept the cards we are dealt, but once we have them in our hands, it is up to us to decide how to play in order to win the game. Athletic success is exactly the same. You have been dealt a hand of cards; how are you going to use them?

There is a method for developing the mechanism of decisive control. Champions do not leave winning to chance. They pursue accomplishment systematically by breaking out of their self-imposed mental prisons and looking at the bright world of possibilities. Losers become prisoners of thousands of restrictions that they have made and applied to themselves. They conform to peer codes; they copy others' training programs, strive toward goals that others have determined for them.

As you read what champion triathletes say about their training, bear in mind that these are the methods that work for them. Decisive control means that you have to make your own decisions about your training and racing plans; only when you accept responsibility for your own training can you accept credit for your victories. The "monkey see, monkey do" training method merely restricts you to the limitations of others. You have to be true to yourself. Until you determine your own goals, you can never meet them.

You can pick out decisive controllers from a crowd of people. They are ready for the race; they know what to expect from life because they have chosen their own course. They don't read their horoscope; they write it. They express freedom of choice—they choose to win.

Each of you holds the tools you need to make the sun shine every day on your own playing field—the field of real life. Each of you will fly as far as you allow yourself to imagine.

MARK GREGORY ALLEN

Hometown: Del Mar, California
Date of birth: January 12, 1958
Height: 6'0"
Weight: 155 pounds
Maximum VO$_2$: ?
Body fat: 6 percent
Current profession: Professional triathlete
Athletic achievements:

Dave Epperson

1982: Nice Triathlon, first place
Horny Toad Triathlon, first place
1983: Nice Triathlon, first place
Bud Light Ironman, third place
1984: Bud Light Ironman, fifth place
Crystal Light New York Triathlon, first place
Nice Triathlon, first place
Gulf Coast Triathlon, first place

In 1984, Mark was undefeated. He won every major pro race:

USTS Tampa
Gulf Coast
Las Vegas
Crystal Light
Nice

Rebecca Gregg

Mark Allen, an athlete renowned for his control.

A MAN REACHING FOR HIS POTENTIAL

I was born in Glendale, California, but we moved to St. Louis for a couple of years when I was four. We lived in an area that was 98-percent black and 2-percent white; it was interesting being in a situation most of my peers will never experience. We didn't live under the best conditions because my dad was going to medical school and didn't have much money. We lived on what my mom earned as a secretary. Our apartment was in a cheap housing project that was horrible; our walls were very thin, and we could hear when the man next door would beat up his wife. There was always urine in the elevators. At night, when my mom came home from work, she had to sit in the car and honk the horn until my dad came out, because we lived on the 12th floor and it was dangerous for a woman to come upstairs alone. Nothing ever happened to her or us, but it's something I won't forget.

After we left St. Louis, we moved to Palo Alto, California. We lived across from Stanford University, where my dad did his residency. I have two younger brothers. One is mentally retarded and goes to Agnews Hospital in Santa Clara. His retardation (Down's syndrome) was a big part of our life as a family, because he required constant

Mark demonstrates how to climb hills out of the saddle.

care. Eventually, we had to put him in a school because we couldn't give him what he needed. My other brother is 17 now and is just getting interested in athletics.

My parents are divorced, but it was a good thing, really. I lived with my mom, and although she went through a couple of years when she needed to get her own life together and didn't have much left over for the kids, she is very happy now and feels good about herself. My mom influenced me a lot in the spiritual sense. She's involved with consciousness-raising activities, and I think a lot of my background comes from her exposure to that. I get my drive and my control from my father.

My interest in sports probably began when I got inspired by watching the '64 Olympics, when Don Schollander and Debbie Meyer were winning gold medals. I was very impressed; that's what motivated me to start swimming. I swam from fifth grade until I graduated from the University of California/San Diego. All that early discipline—swimming for an hour-and-a-half to two hours every night—gave me a good mental base as well as a physical one. I got a lot of inspiration from my fifth-grade teacher. One of the main things I learned from her was that I should think for myself and make my own decisions. She really impressed upon me a sense of my own individuality.

I went to high school in Palo Alto. I was always really small, and I didn't grow tall until I got into the 12th grade, so I never did very well in my swimming until then. I had some problems with self-confidence, and because there were all kinds of expectations in school, swimming became a retreat for me. In the swimming group, everyone was equal and very supportive of each other. There were all kinds of people, but it really made no difference; swimming seemed to bond us. We shared feelings and experiences. I don't feel I gave anything up by spending all that time in the pool—I gained a lot in the form of friendships. Outside of my family, I felt my first closeness to other people in that swimming group.

There was one person who was a very good influence on me in an odd kind of way. His name was Eric Bunje. He and I were "the duo" because we were always doing things together. He had somewhat of a devious mind back then, and I'd always go along with him. Sometimes in a workout, I'd be trying to go as hard as I could, and all of a sudden I'd look down and see Eric sitting on the pool floor making faces at me from under the water. He brought out my fun side. We would always get yelled at by his mom, but it was all part of a game we played to grow up. My time with Eric was a good period in my life.

My swimming improved at the UCSD. I was National Association of Intercollegiate Athletics All-American in about 10 events over a three-year period. I improved because I had grown and become stronger. My degree was in biology, and I got As and Bs with only a few Cs, but it was a struggle for me the whole way through. I'm really glad I got my degree and got it out of the way before picking up the triathlon. I have never used it. I did think about going to medical school, but I wouldn't have been doing that for myself. I knew I had to do something that seemed right for me inside my heart.

After I graduated, I fumbled around for two years. It was a mixed period of good and bad times. I felt free of responsibility and full of possibilities, but at the same time I realized that I couldn't do some of the things I wanted to because I didn't have the money. I traveled

Dave Epperson

Finishing in third place at the 1984 Ironman, Mark Allen.

and surfed in Hawaii and Mexico for a while and enjoyed that a great deal. I watched the 1981 Ironman as my lifeguard friend Reed Gregorson finished fifth. It was Reed who got me excited about the possibility of doing a triathlon. The first race I tried was the USTS San Diego in 1982, where I came in fourth.

Winning the Horny Toad Triathlon (San Diego) was my most exciting athletic accomplishment, because it was the first time that I beat Molina or Tinley. It was also my best event at the time because I felt I had performed as close as I could to my potential. The 1982 Nice Triathlon was similar, but the 1983 race was disappointing from the point of view of reaching my potential. During the race, I became severely dehydrated and was forced to walk. It put racing into perspective for me, finally realizing that my place is not as important to me as is my performance.

ALLEN'S TRAINING:
THE INTENSIVE TRAINING OF A CONSCIOUS MAN

When I first started doing triathlons, it seemed like everybody had a big secret about how they trained. But when I learned exactly what other triathletes were doing, I realized that, while there may be general guidelines that can help younger triathletes just coming into this sport, essentially each person does what works most comfortably for him or her. I consistently do fewer miles than Molina, for example. If I put in as many as he does, I wouldn't be able to put in the intensity that I like to. I get more effect from doing the majority of my workouts at a faster pace than I would if I went out at a moderate pace for a lot more miles. It's just the way I like to train.

It can be hard to push constantly like that, but for me that's where it becomes interesting and fun. I experiment with pain; I concentrate on learning about it and managing it. There's only a certain number of roads I ride on, so I know how fast I'm capable of going. I like to push harder every so often. I like to see what it feels like in my muscles. Does the pain get more intense as I go harder, does it stay the same, or do I find that after I go hard for a while it starts to decrease—or what? All these mental activities keep me from getting stale during training, and they also prepare me for the mental challenge of a race. In any race on any given day, the athlete that is most "with it" mentally is the one who will win. I think most of the top men or women are actually equal in their physical capabilities. It's really whoever is able to focus his mind on what he's doing and who can manage the pain he's going through that will lead the pack.

I can't train year-round. I have an off-season and an on-season. In the middle of winter, Christmas, and the holidays, I don't train very much. I ease into my training in January, and from February on I'm usually building up. I also don't like getting up very early in the morning, so my day starts about 8:00 or 9:00 A.M. In the morning I run, or bike and run, or just bike before I swim. I usually cycle with other people. It's hard for me to go out there day after day by myself, but with other people I am pushed when I don't have the mental energy to push myself. However, cycling with others does have its disadvantages. Sometimes I will feel better than everybody else, so I'll start going hard while they begin to lag behind and talk to each other. Or I might feel awful when the others are ready to do

Dave Epperson

*Mark Allen on his way to defending successfully his Nice Triathlon
championship.*

a hard ride, so I end up hanging on. I usually train with Molina,
Tinley, or Dale Basescu.

I swim at noon in the master's program, and in this sport I usually
need to have someone out there who is as good or better than me to
get me going. I think it's because I've been doing it for so many
years with someone always telling me what to do. I really have to
psyche myself up to swim, so I usually do it four days a week for an

MARK ALLEN'S DAILY TRIATHLON SCHEDULE

		SWIM	BIKE	RUN
MONDAY	Distance:	5,000yds	40mi	
	Time:	1½hrs	2hrs	
TUESDAY	Distance:	5000yds	50mi	12mi
	Time:	1½hrs	2½mi	1¼hrs
WEDNESDAY	Distance:		100mi	6mi
	Time:		5–6hrs	40mins
THURSDAY	Distance:	5000yds	60mi	
	Time:	1½hrs	3hrs	
FRIDAY	Distance:	5000yds	40mi	
	Time:	1½hrs	2hrs	
SATURDAY	Distance:		110mi	
	Time:		5–6hrs	
SUNDAY	Distance:		30mi	15–20mi
	Time:		2hrs	1½–2½hrs

Dave Epperson

Mark Allen working out at the U.C. San Diego pool.

hour-and-a-half each time. I do 5,000 yards; it's all intervals. I'll usually do two sets that have between 2,000 and 3,000 yards in them. I'll do 10 × 200 or 6 × 500 or something similar. Sometimes I'll do 2–3 1,000s. The longest swim I'll do is 1,650 or maybe a 2,000 straight. I like to do a set that fatigues my arms, and the only way I can do that is by doing the hard sets, such as a 2,000 or 3,000 and sometimes by following with another. I use pull buoys and paddles. I usually throw in some pulling, and once in a while I'll kick, which feels good. It loosens up my legs and my mind.

It seems really easy to run on my own, which I usually like to do in the evenings. I do intervals later in the season. I do some track work, and I really like to do fartlek, especially on a 10-or 12-mile run. I get warmed up, push a mile, and then back off, and then I'll do 1–2 miles really hard, get something to drink, and go another 2 miles really hard and so on. I feel I get a lot more from a 10-mile run at a 6-minute average pace if I go some parts at 5:30 and some at 6:30 instead of 6 minutes all the way. As for weight training, I used to do it about twice a week. It definitely adds extra strength.

I eat a lot of high-carbohydrate foods such as cereals, grains, Grape-Nuts, and granola, but not much fat. I eat a little fish and chicken. Every now and then I'll splurge and eat pizza, though I know I shouldn't. The closer I get to a race, the better I eat. For breakfast I'll eat Grape-Nuts or another cereal and a fruit smoothie with nonfat yogurt. After my ride, I might have a salad. Dinner is usually a stir-fry using a Teflon pan without butter. I eat anything I want for dinner. Sometimes I'll even have pancakes. It usually depends on what I feel like I need to eat a lot of. Sometimes I feel like I need carbos, so I'll do that. Other days I'll eat a lot of protein. I take the standard kind of multivitamin daily, but no megadoses, and I take bee pollen in tablet form.

Physically, I can do this sport for another four or five years, but mentally I might be limited. I don't want to grow stale, so I usually think only from year to year in triathlon. I try not to think really too far ahead. I'm hopeful that there will be an increased support and interest in triathlons from the general public, and I hope it will continue to grow like it has. Maybe I will eventually be involved in some kind of promotion of the sport or be able to teach what I have learned in my training to others.

RACING FROM A SENSE OF STRENGTH

I'm not a religious person, but I think I have a religious sense of things in that I really try to be aware of what I do and try not to affect other people negatively. I also like to read philosophical sorts of things—experiences that people have gone through and things they've learned from them. For example, I've read some of Ram

Dave Epperson

Mark crosses the finish line at 1984 Bud Light Ironman.

Dass's work and all of Carlos Castaneda's books. I'll spend days just reading during the off-season. I guess it's a balancing out of the physical intensity required during the rest of the year. It was really refreshing to use a different part of my brain for a while; it got rid of a lot of mental staleness. Those kinds of books have affected my training. Now I really try to be aware of everything that's around me and of the sensations in my body when I'm working out. The more conscious I am of what I'm doing, the less I find myself mentally fatigued. The more I am able to explore new boundaries, the fresher I feel.

Although a little more money makes my life easier, it's not something that brings me the kind of essential happiness that close friends do. To me the most important things in life are the people I'm surrounded by. I don't have 50 great friends, but I have a couple of very close ones and a lot of people I enjoy being with. So, in terms of my motivation for this sport, I couldn't perform anywhere near my potential for money alone. I think most of the people who do races like the Ironman, including myself, do it because they are striving for personal excellence—exclusive of material gain. That's why the race in Nice last year didn't satisfy me. I gained money but no sense of personal accomplishment.

Training and racing offers a chance for me to learn about pushing my body. It's a kind of test. I think this attitude is a lot more positive than the one I used to have. When I used to do well in a race, I got a big confidence boost. This drove me for a while, but I soon learned that that kind of confidence doesn't last. For example, after I won the Horny Toad Triathlon in San Diego, I felt like Superman, but when the feeling went away I was in the same position again. I began to reevaluate my reasons or motives for competing. Was I racing because I wanted to instill confidence in myself by doing well or because I enjoy learning something from pushing my body to its limits? I realized then that racing because you have a need to build your confidence is approaching a challenge from a sense of weakness, whereas racing because I enjoy it is approaching a challenge from a sense of strength.

I think the most interesting race for me is going to be the one in which I'm able to go out and completely disassociate myself from what other people in the race are doing and from worrying about being the first guy in. Trying to go fast enough to beat the other competitors puts a limiting wall around you, and I'd like to break through that barrier; I want to go beyond that and move as fast as my own body is capable of going. They are two different things.

Another thing I've learned, related to first-man confidence, is that the fact that I've completed a race like the Ironman doesn't bestow upon me the ability to do anything I want. I think each set of circumstances in your life is different from what's gone before, and you've got to deal with each new thing as it comes up. When I got off the plane from Nice (1983), I was full of confidence, but when I got to the bus stop, I couldn't find the right bus to get me home. I asked this man—no one special, just an ordinary person—and he knew *exactly* what bus I had to take and what time it would leave. It made me put my win in perspective. A win is irrelevant when I can't find the right bus to go home.

7
MECHANISM 3
ADDICTIVE DISCIPLINE

Triathlons are habit-forming. You find yourself planning improvement strategies for the next race even while you stand exhausted at the finish line of the last one. Each race builds on a previous one and provides you with a stronger base for future events. Each triathlon leads to a renewed commitment to the sport.

As you challenge yourself to reach for new goals, there are certain tools that, if used, will enhance your performance. You already feel burning desire, you probably have decisive control, and your imagination now generates visions of future races in which you see yourself as a winner. But these tools will not advance your fitness level without the application of the mechanism of addictive discipline.

It may appear easy to reprogram your subconscious automaton with a new self-image programming your inner self. But it must be a process of relentless discipline. There are overused expressions about the three most important requirements for success: In business it is "location, location, location"; for musicians the phrase is "rehearse, rehearse, rehearse"; and for triathletes the prescription is "training, training, training." Change occurs like silt settling in a river: it takes layer upon layer of positive reinforcement for success to become the *habit* of success.

Producing change involves addictive discipline, the practice of mental concentration coupled with physical training. Practicing

Dave Epperson

*Working for the American Red Cross in Viet Nam in 1970,
Sally Edwards visits Artillery Base CRB Freedom.*

mental concentration must become part of your daily workout. Exercise psychologists call it "training within," while simultaneously "training without." It is a mental rehearsal of thoughts, emotions, and pictures—your own limitless possibilities.

During 1970–71, I served with the American Red Cross in Viet Nam, along with a group of 100 other American women who were stationed in units throughout the three northern corps. Our assigned task was to raise troop morale by involving the soldiers in recreational programs. We visited forward firebases and grunts in the field, or we would travel by helicopter, landing at LZs. Troops met us in their mess halls, where we would set up recreational programs. Day after day, the American GIs we met were dealing with life and death, boredom and unhappiness.

It was easy to identify the soldiers who were "losers" among the groups assembled in the mess hall. Their appearance was generally scraggly, they lacked esprit de corps, and their talk was full of complaining and bitterness. The "winners," on the other hand, had realized that to survive in harsh war conditions they had to use their time and energy productively. During this period of deprivation and boredom, they used their survival instincts to practice addictive discipline. One soldier would mentally simulate golf, sometimes playing more than one round each day. On the first day back home, he shot par golf after a year of "training within." Others learned computer languages, read the Bible, invented hundreds of money-making ideas, or even shot 100-percent baskets from the free throw line. What these soldiers were doing was training to be the best mentally when they couldn't practice the habit physically. They used the power of imagination to win.

Top athletes do this daily. They mentally practice flawless techniques over and over again. It is the art of simulation, similar to our astronauts' practicing in a spaceship on earth so that when the real space flight occurs it will be identical to their drills.

Addictive discipline creates the winning edge and leads to the attainment of goals. It builds—one layer on another. For me, addictive discipline began with my first marathon in 1976, which I completed, lame, in a time of 4:04. In 1977, I attempted my first 50-miler from Marysville to Sacramento, California. As I crossed the finish line in 7:35, I realized that, if I continued to bite off small chunks and continued to discipline myself, I could run farther. The next year I ran the 75-mile run around Lake Tahoe, finishing in a time of 13:13. Of course, I now had to try 100 miles, so in 1979 I entered the Western States 100-Mile Endurance Run, finishing in third place in 26 hours. The 100-miler led me to my first triathlon, and the same building-up process occurred all over again—one accomplishment after another—until in 1981 I finished the Ironman in 12½ hours, second place.

I have made winning a habit throughout the years, and now I am absolutely addicted to being successful in all my pursuits, through the relentless use of a disciplined attitude.

LINDA ANN BUCHANAN

Hometown:	Davis, California
Date of birth:	May 26, 1957
Height:	5'9"
Weight:	130 pounds
Maximum VO$_2$:	66 ml/kg/min
Body fat:	8 percent
Current profession:	Professional athlete
Athletic achievements:	1982: Sierra Nevada Triathlon, second place
	1983: USTS Los Angeles, first-place woman
	USTS Portland, first place
	Nice Triathlon, first place
	Sacramento Triathlon, first place
	1984: Kauai Loves You Triathlon, first place

A TOMBOY IN DISGUISE

When I was growing up, the one word that described my family was *athletic*. My father went through college on a basketball scholarship, and his team was NCAA champ during his senior year. He now teaches high school and coaches women's basketball. My mother was also sports-oriented, but I remember her as a ballerina, although I'm not sure if that's a true picture. I'm the eldest of four children. We're all very close in age, so we grew up together—in a little group. Because of the closeness, I learned to play basketball and football alongside my two brothers, John and Greg. Greg had asthma and was advised by the doctor to start swimming. He turned out to be an excellent swimmer, and the whole family started swimming, too. I was always in good shape throughout junior high and high school—I played all kinds of different sports.

Although I always dressed nicely, I was actually a tomboy. It was as though I wanted to disguise my athletic prowess until I came down to the tennis court or the baseball diamond. I don't know what motivated me to do that. I'm not sure if that was society's

Linda Buchanan, addicted to athletics.

effect on me or just my own private joke, although I did enjoy surprising everyone.

I stopped swimming when I was about 17. In fact, the whole family stopped because we moved to a town in England where the swimming team swam for only an hour once a week. When we came back I participated in other sports, especially tennis and track. In those days, it was really tennis that I loved most. I wanted to be as good as Chris Evert. It was through my love of tennis that I discovered an inner yearning to be good at something. I even said I wanted to be a professional tennis player. I tried to be good at tennis, but it wasn't really there. I couldn't hit the shot that would make my opponents fall on their faces. Physically I could, but mentally I didn't want to do that. It's interesting to think that I had an idea of being a professional athlete even when I was a teenager.

A week after I started college, my mother was bitten by a spider. Some of her own health problems complicated the situation, and she lost both her legs and all her fingertips. She almost died a couple of times. My parents separated about a year-and-a-half after that. My mom has recovered well and now works at a Dominican college in San Rafael. Sometimes, when I feel sore and wonder, "Why am I doing this?" I think about people like my mother who can't. I do realize how lucky I am.

During my college career, I didn't want to swim competitively, but I swam on my own three times a week. I often would go to the pool and watch the team working out. I joined the crew team, and every day we'd go to Mission Bay and row. I enjoyed that tremendously. I also played on the soccer and tennis teams.

A big turning point came when I joined the swim team again. I gave up all the typical parties and late nights of college life. Returning to swimming in a committed way was really a big step, but the break from disciplined sports had been extremely valuable. I had experimented with and learned about a variety of different sports and actually renewed myself for a period of disciplined commitment toward one sport.

I moved to Davis, California, when I was 21. I thought I wanted to be a PE major, but I found many of the PE classes to be a lot of talk. The first classes I took were on the psychology of sport, and I felt I was being told what I already knew. Since I have always considered sport as something to "do," it was hard to sit down and study it from a book. After one quarter, I left and moved to Lake Tahoe, California.

I taught skiing. Teaching was probably my biggest nonathletic achievement. I consider myself to be an introvert, so you can imagine what an accomplishment it was to stand before a group every day and tell them what to do. But I really enjoyed it.

The 1980 Davis Triathlon was my first individual multi-sport

1983 USTS/Long Beach—Linda Buchanan crossing the finish line in first place.

event. I came in second, seven seconds behind Barbie Bell. My second race was in 1981, and I was in the lead until I got a flat tire. In 1982, I entered another triathlon. After this race, I was definitely a committed athlete.

BUCHANAN'S TRAINING: TRAINING IS NEVER GOING BACKWARD

My weekly schedule is never written down but only tentatively sketched out in my head. I don't train in a structured way; I usually work out how I'm feeling and go from there because I have only a general sense of what I should be doing each week. I don't keep a training log. It makes me too conscious of mileage.

I am both flexible and inflexible in my training habits. For example, I swim every morning. I have to do that. It's a habit that began long before I ever committed myself to triathlons. On the other hand, I'm prepared to vary my weekly pattern according to various intuitions I have about the best way to work out on a particular day. Though I'm flexible in that respect, I always try to make each workout the best one possible at the time. This is where my addictive discipline really reveals itself. I never allow myself to go backward. By that I mean, if I say I'm going to run seven miles, I may do more, but I will never do less. I know if I give in a little bit, it's all gone. I never let up. In this respect, I am in danger of getting injured or of burning out. However, I do know when it is time to take a break, physical or mental.

Generally, my weekly schedule begins with a fairly long run on Sundays. On weekdays I swim every morning; it's usually about 3,500 yards. Afterward, I run between 6 and 10 miles. I run and ride intervals during the week, but again I don't have a set distance or a set time of week when I do that. My minimum bicycle ride is 25 miles, and my long ride is 75–80 miles, usually about once a week. On Saturday I swim about 5,500 yards. I swim/run/bike daily, in that order.

I'm not working with weights at the moment. I do sit-ups and push-ups, but weight training has never sparked my interest. Now I can see that I need the extra strength, so I am going to start using weights again.

As for diet, I've been a vegetarian for eight years. I eat a tremendous amount of carbohydrates and try to avoid sugar, although cookies are my biggest weakness. I don't eat a big breakfast. For lunch I'll eat rice cakes, tofu, fruit. In the evening, if I work, I have a couple of salads and some bread. If I don't, I try to have vegetables and rice or something like that. And then, there are bagels, lots of bagels. I'm very conscious of what I eat.

Dave Epperson

Linda Buchanan astride her Specialized racing bike.

I rely on my own company a great deal when I'm training. When I'm preparing for a race, I mentally simulate a great deal during my training. I play the race out in my mind. I see myself running and biking, and I appear strong and fast; I leave other people out of the image. I also work on concentration—I practice it. If I don't train my concentration, then I can't work hard physically because it's my mental stamina that keeps me going. Working hard physically is identical to working hard mentally. When I decide to ride hard for five miles, I have to mentally trick myself into doing it. The last few days before a race, I really concentrate on eliminating regrets because what hasn't been done before this point, doesn't matter anymore. I don't want to say, "I should have done this," or "I should have done that." Regrets accomplish nothing.

My motivation is really tied up with my refusal to back down— always trying to do more and/or go faster. As I said, I never let myself go backward, and that seems to describe my particular brand of addictive discipline. Even though I'm a professional athlete now and get paid for training and competing in triathlons,

Dave Epperson

Linda Buchanan focuses all of her energy in the 1984 Las Vegas Triathlon.

money is not my motivation. In fact, I probably couldn't exert myself just for dollars. It's a lot more than that, but it's hard to describe exactly. I started training for triathlons because they included things that I liked to do and offered the kind of lifestyle that suited me. I got into the habit of going to the pool every day, and, because I found I liked it and that it enhanced my life, it became a priority. I began to work around that. Whatever works for me seems to become a habit eventually. Habits build on themselves. It seemed to escalate gradually, so that now when I assess myself I see the reality of what I once only imagined myself to be.

I always grew up feeling strong athletically. I never felt inhibited because I was a girl, but still I kept my sense of strength a secret. Now I'm really dealing with myself as a professional female athlete. It has taken me some time to accept myself as a professional.

Some people who may view my life from the outside might see it simply as "repetition and more repetition," however, to me it's all very satisfying. I'm sure I'm addicted to routine. Sometimes I wonder if I'm so disciplined because I'm essentially a lazy person. I don't change very easily. In fact, I don't feel nearly as good about

BUCHANAN WORKOUT SCHEDULE

MONDAY
8:00 A.M.: Swim 3,300–4,000 yards, longer sets (500s to 800s); am usually pretty eager after day off from swimming
10:00 A.M.: After breakfast, run 5–6 miles, slow and easy, working on consistent pace
1:00 P.M.: Bike 35 miles, start easy, return hard, even pacing

TUESDAY
8:00 A.M.: Swim 3,500 yards, short sets, short rest intervals
10:00 A.M.: Run 8–10 miles, out easy, pick up last 4 miles
1:00 P.M.: Bike 50 miles, push middle third in hills

WEDNESDAY
8:00 A.M.: Swim 3,500 yards
10:00 A.M.: After breakfast, run 7 miles, fartlek ½ miles
12 NOON: Bike 40 easy miles

THURSDAY
8:00 A.M.: Swim 3,500 yards
10:00 A.M.: Bike 75 miles immediately followed by a short run (1–2 miles) to work on transition

FRIDAY
Started to get a little fatigued by this time of the week, so I took an easy day:
8:00 A.M.: Swim 3,500 yards
10:00 A.M.: Bike 35 miles
12 NOON: Run 10 easy miles

SATURDAY
7:00 A.M.: Run 4–5 miles
8:30 A.M.: Swim 5,500 yards
10:30 A.M.: Bike 50 miles hard, with whatever is left
All done with as little in-between time as possible.

SUNDAY
Run 13–18 miles with a friend.

This was a typical training week a month prior to Nice. I know working out seven days a week is generally not recommended, but I found it to be suitable for me. However, occasionally a day off would be needed (either for mental or physical reasons)—I probably averaged 2–3 days per month. This would be taken whenever needed as opposed to a scheduled day off.

Dave Epperson

Linda Buchanan passes Joanne Ernst to win the 1984 Las Vegas Triathlon.

myself if I haven't gone through my little routines. Often I'll hold little "carrots" out to myself, yet when I find myself in the position to take them, I rarely want them.

I think another part of addictive discipline is hardly ever feeling bored. I can entertain myself very well. Working out is rarely repetitious or boring to me because I'm always working on my mind as well as my body. I don't let my mind wander. I practice being mentally stronger by never giving up or backing down.

There are drawbacks to all the training. I usually go to bed early, so I end up losing out on some social activities. I can't always do things that other people want to do. Overall, I have gained far more than I've lost, and every day, through consistent discipline, I conquer a little more fear. I'm trying to put a lot of fear behind me, and, although I still have a lot left, I don't let it stop me from trying. I keep moving forward. The one thing I'm certain about is being disciplined—that's the quality that sets me apart from others.

8

TOOL 4

DEEP-DOWN CONFIDENCE

I had run the best race of my life, a 100-miler across the Sierra Nevada, in 1980. We had started in Squaw Valley and ended in Auburn, California. I had set a goal to win, trained to win, and knew that I could. Sure enough, after following a carefully designed plan and with tremendous support from others, I won. It took 22 hours of nonstop running at a work load measured at 85-percent heart rate. Fifteen minutes after I had crossed the line, the second woman arrived, Bjorg Austrheim-Smith. I stood up, which was difficult because my legs were shot, hobbled over to the finish line, and applauded Bjorg as she came across. It had always seemed to me that the only way that you can break the tape first is if everyone else is behind; therefore, you have to thank and honor those who have helped you win.

Immediately after finishing, Bjorg, clearly with more energy, accepted a bottle of champagne from her handlers. Then she came over to where I was sitting, waving her finger in my face and saying, "Next year, Edwards, I am going to beat you." She turned away, and I shook my head in amazement.

The next year, the 1981 Western States 100-Miler was a faster event. A film crew shot the contest for national television, and we raced our hearts out. We traded the lead several times. This time, I crossed the finish line two hours faster, and Bjorg, well, she crossed the line three-and-a-half hours faster. The tables had turned. As the second-place winner, I found her in the crowd and thanked her for the race. By thanking her, I learned how much self-confidence it requires to recognize that she was, that day, the stronger and swifter athlete.

Being able to say, "Thank you," is one of the numerous traits of someone who has deep-down confidence. Responding to a compliment with sarcasm announces one's insecurity. When you belittle yourself, your automaton, your subconscious self-image, believes that what you say out loud is true and stores it as reality. By demeaning yourself, you are really teaching yourself that you do not deserve to be a winner.

The words *deep-down confidence* literally mean a belief in your abilities and powers as a source that lies at your center. It is a type of self-reliance that is based on believing in the worth of the self and trusting in it. Deep-down confidence is one of your most important qualities, one you develop into a habit by practicing and internalizing. It is a lifetime developmental process.

Have you ever noticed athletes who don't quite live up to their potential? Though they may have one good race, they never win a string of victories. They have the genetic ability but are low achievers. They have untapped ability but have learned the habit of concentrating on their failures; their self-talk reinforces a losing cycle. Self-confidence is built on the experience of success. Winners know that they will lose some contests but that it doesn't matter how many failures there are in the past; short-time disappointments should serve as corrective feedback. But it can destroy deep-down confidence if it negatively imprints on the automaton.

Self-confidence comes from knowing that the grass is green on *both* sides of the fence. Winners take pride and pleasure in their current professions, relationships, and athletic accomplishments. Successful athletes dig within and mine their assets, accepting themselves in the moment, knowing that self-improvement will follow. They are willing to accept responsibility for their actions and thoughts. Shakespeare says the same thing in *Hamlet*:

This above all: to thine own self be true,
And it must follow, as the night the day,
Thou canst not then be false to any man.

Deep-down confidence in your "center" is perpetuated by self-talk. Athletes practice positive self-talking to reinforce the winning cycle. Researchers know the power of words, that they can control bodily functions through biofeedback. Your thoughts can raise your body temperature, secrete hormones, dilate and constrict arteries, and raise and lower pulse rate. Words can also change your

Hughes Photography

*Sally Edwards running in
the 1980 Western States
100 Mile ultramarathon
setting a course record of
20 hours and 7 minutes.*

deep-down sense of confidence. Successful athletes use positive feedback through such self-talk phrases as "I can," "I look forward to," "I'm feeling better," " I'll do it better."

In contrast, losers frequently put themselves down with self-talk phrases that continue to program the automaton. They use phrases such as "I can't," "I won't," "I should have," "I might have," "I did terribly."

Without exception, real stars—whether in athletics, business, or other activities—*like* themselves; they have accepted their own uniqueness and enjoy their sense of difference. One of the ways to distinguish a star from an also-ran is by the fact that successful people naturally attract friends and supporters—they rarely stand alone.

Nor will you. Through the door of your own deep-down confidence lies the tool of athletic success and happiness.

JULIE MOSS

Hometown:	Carlsbad, California
Date of birth:	October 15, 1958
Height:	5'5½"
Weight:	120 pounds
Maximum VO$_2$:	67 ml/kg/min
Body fat:	8–10 percent
Current profession:	Professional athlete

Athletic achievements:

1982: Bud Light Ironman, second place

1983: Malibu Triathlon, first place
USTS San Diego, first place
Rio de Janiero Triathlon, first place

1984: Nice Triathlon, second place
Crystal Light New York Triathlon, second place
USTS San Diego, second place
Bonne Bell Triathlon, first place

Julie is known as one of the most fun-loving triathletes on the circuit. She congratulates Renee Thomas at the finishline.

Dave Epperson

Julie Moss.

A NATURAL ATHLETE

I was born in Pomona, California. My parents divorced when I was a fourth-grader, and my mother moved my brother and me down to the beach because she felt it would be a healthier environment for us to grow up in. We were on our own a lot during that time because my mother needed to go to school in order to eventually support us. In addition to teaching, my mom needed to finish her Master's degree in education at night school. We didn't see very much of my father after the divorce. He really hasn't been very involved in our lives.

My father was a natural athlete, and I'm sure I inherited that from him because I have a great deal of natural endurance, and I can usually pick up any sport and have fun with it without feeling frustrated. As a teenager, I was definitely a tomboy; but I enjoyed being different from the other girls in that way. Somehow, I realized that to be a tomboy was actually a healthy thing. I surfed a lot, and I loved being the only girl out there. During my high school years, I would choose a new sport every year. I went from basketball to softball and from volleyball to tennis. I enjoyed changing my interests even though I was always on the B teams and sometimes on the bench. I was never "the best."

During college I was fairly nonathletic, although I started jogging and still surfed. I ran a half-marathon, but I was primarily moti-

Dave Epperson

Julie Moss receives aid at the Bahamas Triathlon.

vated to do it because I had a mad crush on this boy who was running in it, too, and it was a chance to get to know him.

Overall, I didn't apply myself in college, although the teachers used to tell me that if I had, I would have gotten better grades. Instead, I tended toward adventure and would rush off to Mammoth for a week of skiing or to Mexico for surfing.

Probably the major athletic influence for me came from Reed Gregerson. He was the athletic turning point in my life. I called him a "Renaissance man" because he is gifted in so many different areas. It was because he talked about the Ironman so much that I decided to participate in it myself.

A fairly recent event in my life has been my mother's remarriage to a great man. He and my mother have been to the last two Ironmans and have become a real support unit for me when I race.

Probably my greatest athletic achievement was placing third in the 1983 Bass Lake USTS Championships. I felt I was in the best shape possible, and it was also my first experience of really competing against the best. It was actually a psychological accomplishment because I peaked for the race.

MOSS'S TRAINING:
TRAINING IS OCCASIONALLY DOING SOMETHING WILD

I'm definitely applying myself to my training, but I'm not one of those people who is continually effortful and puts in a lot of tedious hours for the sake of success. I admire those people, but I'm not one of them. Occasionally, I like to switch gears and do something wild. Luckily, triathlons have been a vehicle for me to travel and explore and do things that are totally non-triathlon-oriented. I've used triathlons to pay for trips to South America, and because of my exposure in Ironman, I was invited to New Zealand for an athletic competition and remained for a month-long bike tour.

I don't follow a strict diet. Now and then I eat fish and chicken and a little beef if someone else cooks it for me, but usually I eat vegetarian meals. I'm also on Dr. Colgan's personalized vitamin program. (He runs the Colgan Institute of Nutritional Science in Carlsbad, California.)

My short-term goals are to break 37:30 in a 10k run, ride a 25-mile time trial in one hour flat, and consistently perform in a pool. I'd like to push for shorter races where the average athlete can get out and compete in a triathlon. For this, I'm committing myself to do a lot of clinics next year and a great deal of guest speaking, triathlon camps, and showing up at local and national races. My starts in triathlons are largely due to efforts of the USTS people. They believed in me and I believe in their series.

As for long-term goals, I'm committed to triathlons on a year by year basis. I also want to do well at the Ironman. I eventually want to move out of competition into the promotion of the sport. In addition, I'm attempting to earn a degree in sports psychology. Basically, the idea behind getting this degree is to encourage the average person to become excited about sports and to start partic-ipating. I want to incorporate this into some kind of media-based work because the media reach a bigger audience than I can reach in a clinic.

I have a lot of energy, a good sense of humor, and I truly enjoy other people. I do have a strong sense of my own uniqueness. Now I'm beginning to express things about myself that I've felt were in me but weren't always evident. I think I am usually perceived as just being bubbly and enthusiastic and out for a good time, but I keep progressing, and the sustaining power to do that has to come from somewhere else, from within.

I think my confidence is partially a result of my childhood independence and also because my mother always insisted that I could become whatever I wanted to become. Confidence, in general, also comes from knowing you've done a good job at whatever you've chosen to do. You feel good about yourself, and

TRAINING SCHEDULE—JULIE MOSS

MONDAY

Morning: Run easy four miles to Nautilus club and work out for 30-45 minutes. Run home.

Afternoon: Swim (4,000-5,000 yards) in UCSD Masters program. I need the discipline and motivation of a coach. I also need the peer pressure of friends knowing if I miss a workout.

Evening: Ride two hours easy.

TUESDAY

Morning: Swim (4,000-5,000 yards) with Carlsbad Masters, once a week.

Afternoon: Run intervals with running group, "Magic Bullets," out near UCSD.

Evening: Easy ride, 2-3 hours.

WEDNESDAY

Morning: With group, long ride (90-100 miles). Easy run (4-5 miles) and Nautilus club workout (30-45 minutes).

THURSDAY

Morning: Long hilly run and then ride for two hours.

Afternoon: Masters swim (see Monday).

FRIDAY

Morning: Run 10-11 miles easy and ride for two hours.
Afternoon: Masters swim (4,000-5,000 yards)

Evening: Nautilus workout (30-40 minutes)

SATURDAY

Long group ride for 80-100 miles and an easy run (4-8 miles).

SUNDAY

If not racing 10k or half marathon, then long run 15 miles hard and an easy ride (1-2 hours).

COMMENTS

Logs: I never really kept a log until recently, and it has proven very helpful. Numbers don't lie! A log becomes your conscience.

Opting for a Speedo swimsuit rather than a trisuit, Julie Moss is one of the sport's strongest cyclists.

Racing: I'm doing both USTS and off-road bike racing as part of my training. Between running and cycling, I can race two days out of a week, and that keeps me sharp. As soon as you add racing to your training, you separate out the pleasure element and tend to work even harder. And when it's time to compete in a triathlon, some of the fear of competition is gone.

then you feel good about other people. As for people, I feel that everyone I meet in this sport has something to offer me. I try to give that back, so an energy is established among all of us.

Confidence builds on itself. You think enough of yourself to get out there and do a workout. You accomplish the workout and feel good about that. Further on, you enter a race knowing you've done the best job preparing that you can do. You do well in the race, and so it goes on. Confidence is a self-fulfilling thing. You start out small. You can't think of yourself as the best triathlete in the world. You need to humble yourself and realize that essentially you're no *better* than any other person in the race but that you are *different*. Then your self-esteem builds, because you realize you're doing something that everybody else could do, and you're working very hard at it.

I think my confidence is reflected in my positive attitude. I accept what I really can't change about myself; I have red hair and freckles, and I'll never be able to get a good tan. On the other hand, I don't accept anything that bothers me if it is possible to change it. I take the attitude that, if I'm not running well enough, it's because I'm not training hard enough, so I try to improve on my training.

As to changing what can be changed, I think there are pros and cons in trying to perfect oneself. Right now I'm going through a stage where I feel I want to be the best person I can be. It encompasses a thousand different facets of myself. But really, if you spend all day trying to be perfect, your life can become rather dull.

In a race, I'm not completely doubt-free, but I think my stronger side usually comes through. We all have doubts caused by these new women triathletes who are coming into the sport, but I use those doubts to my advantage. They're fuel for my fire. Every time a doubt comes in, I have tons of rationalizations and ammunition to fight it off. I'm very easy to boost, too. Usually it just takes one person to come by and say, "Oh, Julie, I'm so glad to meet you. I've always wanted to meet you," and I feel belong in triathlons. Everyone experiences doubt, but the difference lies in how you deal with it.

I felt I dealt with doubt in my characteristic way in that now-famous finish in the 1982 Ironman. I remember it so clearly. I thought, "What is the big deal? I can finish the race. Sure my legs are going out on me, but I'm a long way from being wiped out." Despite my physical condition and that need to get to a bathroom in the last mile, there was no doubt in my mind that I would finish the race, and I just kept going. Maybe that was where my confidence was asserting itself.

Another example of how I fight doubts in a positive way can be

Dave Epperson

***On the Kona-Kailu highway running the marathon stage of the BUSTS,
Julie Moss.***

seen in my preparation for the same 1982 Ironman. I had been
training for it with Reed when we broke up. So then I had to decide
if I was doing the training for Reed or for myself. Probably a little
of both. All these doubts about motivation came in, but I used
whatever motivation needed to get me over there.

I was literally on my own for a whole month before the race. I was
meeting other people and discussing training methods and so on,
but it was really the first time I've been on my own with a set goal.

In a race like that, everyone is on her own throughout the actual event and has moments of "Who am I? What am I doing here?" It's very much a soul-searching adventure. You have to dig down and keep on going, but the nice thing is you see everyone else going through the same experience.

I had some incredible moments during which I've never pushed so hard, and I wonder now if I'll ever push that hard again. But it's amazing how you look back, and you don't feel the pain, although you remember that some very intense things happened. If you're athletic and you think you'd enjoy something like that, the Ironman is one of the most intense, wonderful things you could ever do. It's a peak experience, and that's why I really recommend it.

9
MECHANISM 4
DOUBLE-WIN SPIRIT

The only way that I can win is if you win. The only way that you can win is if I win. That is the expression of a competitive athletic attitude that is both positive and antithetical to the football-playing mentality that says, "I have to hurt you," and "The only way I can score is over your dead body."

The double-win spirit is founded on the view that your opponent is your best friend and a person who forces you to be better, who sets the standard and helps fire your desire to excel. An athlete who practices the double-win spirit doesn't stand victoriously over a beaten enemy but instead thanks a competitor for being there. Practicing a double-win spirit means extending your strong hand to one that is reaching for help, sharing with others, and helping even one more person live a better life. The double-win person knows that if he or she helps you win, then you both win.

The single-win philosophy is "Do unto others before they do unto you." What follows is the "For me to win, you have to lose" attitude.

There is more to the double-win spirit than helping your competitor. Double-winners understand the value of time; they know that, once time is spent, it is gone. The rapid passage of time can be appreciated quickly on the triathlon turf. There are no time-outs during transitions or at fluid stations, no substitutions if your tire flats or you dehydrate, and no penalty box if you break the rules or need a rest. The clock is running, right now, always. If you're not

One of the pre-race rituals before the clock starts to run.

out training, your competition is. Life's not a training workout that fills a vast time void. Life *is* the race, and we must try to squeeze the most from it. When time is gone, it is gone forever. We can't make it up.

An experience that illustrates the double-win spirit happened to me in the 1982 Ironman. After 10½ hours of fierce competition and with one mile to the finish line, I reeled in Kathleen McCartney, the previous year's champion. She was at the end of her rope, staggering, with the ABC "Wide World of Sports" cameras on her every step, anticipating the fall-and-crawl finish. As I caught up with her, I slowed down and said, "Kathleen, I want to run with you to the finish line." Her head lifted, a faint smile came across her lips, and she said, "Yes, Sally, I want to run with you, too." Her stride quickened, but after 20 yards she had to walk again. Her leg-muscle glycogen was shot, but her will was strong. "You want to break 11 hours, don't you?" she asked. I nodded. "Then you have to leave," she said. "I can't run; I can only walk."

Dave Epperson

Ardis Joan Bow.

I left the fallen champion to continue with my own race against time. I knew that by giving her some of my energy she would return it to me a hundred times over. I crossed the finish line in third place: 11 hours, 3 minutes. Kathleen followed nearly eight minutes later, walking tall, her head high. Both of us were double-winners.

ARDIS JOAN BOW

Hometown:	Sacramento, California
Date of birth:	January 20, 1956
Height:	5'5"
Weight:	120 pounds
Maximum VO$_2$:	68 ml/kg/min
Body fat:	8 percent
Current profession:	Professional athlete and portrait artist
Athletic achievements:	1982: Bud Light Ironman World Championship, sixth place Nice Triathlon, fifth place 1983: Ultimate Endurance Triathlon, third place 1984: Big Island Triathlon, first place Oxford International Triathlon, second place Ultimate Endurance Triathlon, first place Holland International Triathlon, first place

ARTIST AND ATHLETE— ANOTHER DOUBLE WIN

Although I was born in the Bethesda, Maryland, Naval Hospital, I spent my first few years of life in Falls Church, Virginia. My father was a career naval officer; my mother was an interior decorator.

I am the fifth of six children, and the only one with a passion for either sports or art. I am a blend of both my mother's and father's interests. My dad played basketball and ran track throughout high

Dave Epperson

Ardis stops for a moment during a training ride, and appreciates the environment.

school and college. My mother, a member of the American Pen Women (a national organization of artists, writers, poets etc.), has drawn, painted, and designed for as long as I can remember. She has always exhibited a tremendous amount of energy and enthusiasm, having raised six energetic children. She strives for perfection in all that she does.

My athletic endeavors started at the age of three, when I fell into the neighbor's pool while reaching for a floating beach ball. Although there were adults at poolside, they evidently thought I was in no great danger. I floundered to the edge of the pool, and water has been in my veins ever since. My astrological sign, Aquarius, is water, not to mention that in the Icelandic language the name *Ardis* means "Ferry over water." My competitive career started with age-group swimming in the eight-and-under category. Unfortunately, because of the military rotation schedule, we did not always live near a pool with a swimming program; therefore, I stopped swimming completely for five years.

Ironically, it was the military life that got me back into the sport of swimming as well as tennis. In 1970, my father took a tour of duty in the Canal Zone, Panama. This was my first experience living on a military base with an Olympic-size pool and tennis courts. I took up both swimming and tennis with great zeal. Having just missed the competitive season in swimming, I trained for the next year on my own. Swimming victories became my forte.

In 1973, my family moved to Seattle. John Denver's "Rocky Mountain High" was at the top of the charts, so I donned my hiking boots and started trekking. Always attacking new adventures in a big way, I started with a climb to the summit of Mt. Rainier—14,500 feet. I spent my senior year attempting the major peaks—Mount Adams, the Brothers, and Mount St. Helens, may she rest in "pieces."

My first two years of college were spent at Central Washington University, where I joined the women's competitive swimming program and started running. Prior to that time I had a great distaste for running, so I enrolled in a jogging class to ensure a consistent routine. My exam at the end of the class was to run a 14-minute 2-mile for an *A* grade. That was so easy that the following day I started running 6 miles daily. I now profess the point of view that, if you can run 2 miles, you can run 6; if 6, then 10; if 10, then 26; if 26; then 50, and so on. As competitive swimming became less important to me (in my junior year), I took up long-distance running, averaging 10–15 miles per day. Meanwhile, I had transferred to the University of Hawaii, where the environment was more conducive to dual-sport workouts.

In March of 1979, I visited my nephew on Catalina Island, where

I had worked and run trails during the summer of 1977. Although I did not have the proper mileage under my belt for a 26-miler, I decided to enter the Catalina Island Marathon; my memories of the beauty of the course were too enticing. I vowed to complete the marathon even if I had to walk to do so.

The prerace strategy paid off, and I conquered the rugged mountain terrain (6,000 feet of elevation change) in 4:28. I discovered a new love: trails and long distance. The following year I entered my first ultramarathon, a 62-miler, finishing in just under 8 hours. I also set a U.S. age record for 100k with a time of 10 hours.

When I graduated from the University of Washington in 1978 with an *A* in art, I realized I had an enormous appetite for new competitive athletic endeavors. My best friend gave me a green Bianchi, and I turned to the triathlon. Like others, I read a *Sports Illustrated* article on the Bud Light Ironman. In February 1982, I made the journey to Hawaii with a solid background in swimming and running and absolutely no experience with a 10-speed. My goal was survival.

I placed 11th that year and gained tons of experience and awareness. I realized that I wanted to train toward reaching my full athletic potential in the triathlon. There is a mental toughness in each sport that doesn't automatically cross over to the other two. At that first Ironman, I really felt like a novice triathlete; I had so much to learn and so far to grow. I still do. It's exciting to know that I have a tremendous amount of yet-untapped potential. I've been racing triathlons now for three years, usually finishing as the bridesmaid but always meeting with success. My race forte is definitely in the long and ultradistances. I really believe that you have to specialize in one or the other. I race the sprint triathlons to keep an edge.

I put far more emphasis on the mental than the physical aspect of training, the area of training I think is virtually ignored by most athletes. I am extremely tough mentally. My long-range athletic goals are to race competitively in the triathlon at least another five years. My mental and physical training will become more balanced. In past training, I have slacked off my swimming workouts and put my emphasis first on the bike, then on the run. Today my skills are more evenly developed, and I'm putting equal emphasis on all three.

It was during my adventures in ultradistance running that I developed my "win-win" attitude. Knowing that I would be engaged in the same activity for up to 10 hours with the same people, I realized that to concentrate on only the positive and to share that with others was the most rewarding way for me to cross the finish line. With a win-win spirit, you can walk away at the end of each race with the biggest trophies in life—very special friends and memories. I know that one of the keys to happiness is to give of

Dave Epperson

Ardis Bow races on off-terrain bikes, too.

yourself and to give unconditionally. Two of my favorite authors explain:

"If life's meaning is to be discovered, it is intrinsic in each stage as we assume the challenge of actualizing every moment of every day as we live it."—Leo Buscaglia

"The purpose of life is to live it, to taste experience to the utmost, to reach out eagerly and without fear for newer and richer experience."—Eleanor Roosevelt

I started practicing double-winning by saying something encouraging to anyone who passed me or whom I passed in my races. I found that, by doing this, I created positive energy and that, when I gave energy, I received greater amounts in return. This is the double-win spirit—this newfound energy for myself and energy to be shared by those willing to take it. If I give to you or if I can help you, by doing so, I am actually helping myself. If I help you win, then I win. As the proverb says: "When you create other winners like yourself, life will pay you back and shine its sun upon your face and put the wind at your back."

BOW'S TRAINING:
TRAINING FOR THREE SEASONS—FALL/WINTER, SPRING, AND SUMMER

My training is broken up into three seasons. In the winter season—November through February—I try to break from the triathlon routine of swim/bike/run. This period of time is busiest for my freelance art business, so I put my priorities in that direction. As far as training goes, I enjoy the discipline I've developed on my Powercam "Road Machine." All my winter mileage is performed on that apparatus; it's a love/hate relationship that I really benefit from. I spend almost no time in the water because I hate getting cold. However, I plan to change that attitude this winter. My running mileage stays about the same throughout the year, with an emphasis on running races throughout the winter. This is the time

ARDIS BOW TRAINING LOG
1984

Day	Date	Sport	Rating	Distance	Time	Pulse	Hours Sleep	Commentary
S	9/1	Swim	7	3000	45m		7 hrs	easy
		Bike	8	80mi	5hr			Easy ride some hills heat
M		Run	6	9mi	1:20		8 hrs	Easy run with friends
		Bike	9	25mi	1hr			Turbo train work on spin
T							7hrs	
		Swim	7	3500	45mn			Intervals 5x200 2:45
		Run	10	9mi	1:30			Speed work 4x1mi repeats
W		Bike	8	110mi	7hrs		8hrs	long ride easy heat train
		Swim	7	4000	1hr			easy worked on mechanics
T		Run	6	8mi	1hr		8 hrs	
		Bike	9	35mi	1:30			15 easy warm 10 hard 5 easy
F		Run	9	7-8mi	1:30		7½hrs	hills hard up easy down
		Swim	8	3500	1hr			Intervals 10x100 1:15
S		Race Run	10	13.1mi	1:38		6½hr	Silver State Half not enough fluids started out slowly then picked up pace
	Total For Week			Swim 14,000	Bicycle 250	Run 46	Sleep 52 hours	Good week will rest up for world's toughest in Tahoe.

Weight __119__ Average For Week
Week No. _____ Year — To Date

TRIATHLON LOG, Fleet Feet Press (916) 442-7223.

ARDIS BOW'S WEEKLY TRIATHLON TRAINING ROUTINE

	RUN	**SWIM**	**BIKE**
Monday	5:30–7:00 A.M. 1½ hours, 7–9 miles easy with a half-mile pickup in the middle	8:00–8:45 P.M. 2,500 yards: 500 swim, 500 kick, 5 × 200 interval, 500 paddles	Powercam "Road Machine"
Tuesday	5:30–6:30 P.M. Speed work, 8–9 miles; 4 × 1-mile, repeat ½-mile, cool between 1-mile warm-up and cool-down at the end	7:30–8:30 P.M. 3,500 yards: 1,000 swim, 500 kick, 3 × 200 4 × 100, 500 paddles, 500 swim	
Wednesday		7:00–8:00 P.M. 3,000 yards: 1,000 swim, 1,000 paddles, 500 kick, 500 swim	3:30–6:30 P.M. 50 miles, 60–65 percent rolling hills
Thursday		8:30–9:00 P.M. 1,500 stretch, easy	6:30–8:00 P.M. 35 miles: 10 mile warm-up, 15 mile time trial, 10 mile cool down

Friday	5:30–6:30 A.M. hilly 6–7 miles. Hard up, recovery down	Powercam, ½ hour
Saturday	Race or long bike, 100 miles	
Sunday	Race or long run, 15–20 miles	

One of my goals is to organize my time enough for the most consistent workout schedule possible. For the most part, I set up on a weekly basis. Because of my profession, my work load fluctuates, depending on deadlines. However, I do like to make myself available to phone or work during the normal working hours. I normally work out before 8:00 and after 5:00; this way there are always a lot of people to train with. Primarily, I try to fit the long, hard, easy theory into my program: On a weekly basis I will schedule one long day or hard day and one easy day in each discipline, but not all on the same day. For example:

Monday	Run easy	Swim hard
Tuesday	Run hard	Bike easy
Wednesday	Swim hard	Bike long
Thursday	Run easy	Swim long
Friday	Run long	Bike easy
Saturday	Swim easy	Bike hard

My training intensity varies throughout the year. I take time off during the late fall through winter to concentrate on my other interests and activities.

I run, work a little on weights, and periodically ride the stationary bike just enough to keep my sanity and to keep my weight down.

There are a couple marathons that I like to run during the winter months.

Dave Epperson

Bow was an accomplished ultramarathoner before she changed her focus toward triathlons.

when I take on other activities that interest me, such as tennis and skiing. If I would put an emphasis on any one facet of training for winter, it would be working with weights to build strength.

Spring brings the first triathlon races of the new season. My emphasis for this period of training is on endurance. Along with my weight work and Racer-Mate training, I add rowing for variety, swimming—brrr!—and, finally, getting out on the road again on *two* wheels!

That brings me into the racing season. I enjoy the long or ultradistance races the most, so I arrange my schedule accordingly. During this phase I work on technique and fine tuning. Because I like the long ones, I don't train as intensely as in the spring, giving myself adequate recovery time between events. I rest a day or two before each long race and the same amount after the event. I don't think ultras take any more time as far as training goes, but I have to make sure I eat and sleep and rest well for the next few days after an event to rebuild my strength. By rest, I mean totally backing off for two days, with the exception of easy swimming. In my experience, it is better to do nothing than to continue training while fatigued—recovery time is much faster. What you really want to steer clear of is injury or illness, which will set you back the furthest.

10

TOOL 5
KEEN AWARENESS

The question people most frequently ask me is, "Why do you do it? Why do you run 100 miles, race the Bud Light Ironman, tackle the Levi's Ride and Tie, challenge the Ultimate Endurance Triathlon?"

At first there doesn't seem to be a very good answer. The classic responses, such as, "Because it is there" or "To see if I can finish it," just don't suffice.

Probably the clearest way to explain my reasoning is through an experience that occurred during the Western States 100-Miler in June 1981. A television crew had requested and received permission from race officials to film the story of my race across the Sierra Nevada Mountains from Squaw Valley to Auburn. The trail is rugged and accessible by car only at certain points. Whenever they could, "PM Magazine," with Richard Hartz and crew, would meet me, asking how I felt and the same repetitive question: "Why do you run 100 miles?" At first I was irritated because there was so much more that was happening than the search for motive and explaining that I felt progressively worse.

But I knew what they were searching for, and, as I ran with all my heart to reach that finish line, I reached further and further inside myself and discovered my center. It is an amazing feeling to touch who you really are, to reach down deep and communicate with the personal place that is you.

That is the reason. I want to become more aware of who I am, to learn about and understand myself. That is the reason I challenge

A new awareness on taking water at an aid station.

Dave Epperson

Sally Edwards (left) and Holly Beattie winning the 1983 Levi Ride & Tie with "Little Art," their endurance Arabian steed.

the distance, the clock, the race, the individual—because I want to know (not know about) the real Sally Edwards. I touched my soul that day.

In our day-to-day existence, we are protected from knowing our real selves by layers and layers of "other" selves. We have developed temporary artifices in order to avoid touching our centers. In meditation, prayer, or deep thought, some people can find a path that leads to their deepest, innermost self. But for me, it is only when my body has reached its physical limits that my mind will allow me to discover that sense of who I am. One's real self occupies a place that many people fear to find, and yet the peace that comes from knowing is worth the journey.

That is what keen awareness is. It is knowing who you are, what you believe in, what your great, personal potential is—and what future roles and goals lie ahead in order to attain fulfillment. Experiences such as the Ironman Triathlon allow you an opportunity to learn these things. They add to your knowledge of self by utilizing your inherent insight, self-feedback, and judgment. Keen awareness is characterized by extreme honesty.

Honesty starts with yourself. You have to be honest about your potential and what it takes to reach it. You have to confront the time and effort it takes to reach your potential. Honesty then spills over into every other aspect of your life, into your business or profession, and into other people's confidence in you.

The foundation stones that we must build on in developing ourselves to our greatest potential are truth, integrity, and honesty. All three must be developed for any real success to occur and to last. Keen awareness means seeking, understanding, and training with truth in our everyday lives.

Practitioners of keen awareness are sensitively tuned in to others and to their own environment. They are open to new opportunities and to learning about their potential to grow and contribute to the best qualities of life. They are open-minded. They realize that each of us has equal rights to fulfill our potential and to be treated as worthy of respect regardless of sex, birthplace, religion, financial status, or intelligence.

Sure enough, everyone hears a different drummer, sees through a different set of lenses. You are unique. There is not one single individual here today, there yesterday, or coming tomorrow that is your clone. But champions understand each individual's uniqueness and accept the differences. This acceptance is empathy; it means running in another's shoes before passing judgment. It is watching a marathon and feeling your legs ache, watching a bike spill and feeling the way the rider feels when he or she tries to stand. Empathy is getting inside someone else and evaluating yourself through that person's eyes.

One of the best examples of newfound empathy is told by Eva Oberth-Ueltzen, third-place finisher of the 1983 Bud Light Ironman. She was there when Julie Moss crawled across the finish line in the Ironman and on TV screens all across America. Eva said: "I was embarrassed for Julie. I felt sympathy for her. She should have paced herself better. I can't imagine ever going that far into exhaustion. I would never do that." The very next year, Eva was in the lead of the Sacramento Triathlon on a hot June day. As she approached the finish line, only 100 yards away, the world began to spin, her knees collapsed, and everything went dark. The next thing she remembers is waking up in a hospital bed. "That was my first helicopter ambulance ride, and I don't remember any of it," she later commented. After four bottles of IV fluid, Eva recalled how she had felt sympathy for Julie Moss before. On her hospital bed that same sympathy turned to empathy. She had raced in Julie's shoes; she now sees and judges the others differently.

There will be or has already been a moment of truth for you. It is the experience that leads you to the first few steps of self-development. It is the day you learned how much potential you have, how many personal assets you possess, and how you have to challenge yourself. Your moment of truth might start with these pages, quitting a race, having a child, or any one of a number of other experiences. It will suggest to you who you are and start you on the path toward developing and using your quality of keen awareness.

DAVID F. SCOTT

Hometown: Davis, California
Date of birth: April 19, 1954
Height: 6'0"
Weight: 164 pounds
Maximum VO$_2$: 74 ml/kg/min
Body fat: 7 percent
Current profession: Professional triathlete, coach
Athletic achievements:

1980: Bud Light Ironman, first place
1982: Bud Light Ironman, first place
1983: Bud Light Ironman, first place
1984: Bud Light Ironman, first place

Dave Epperson

Dave Scott, four-time winner of the Ironman Triathlon.

Dave Epperson

En route to setting an Ironman marathon record of 2:53.

HOMETOWN BOY MAKES GOOD

My childhood was typical, really nothing special. I was born in Woodland, California, because there wasn't a hospital in my hometown of Davis. But I went to grammar school, high school, and college in Davis—and now I live there. Davis is home to me.

As a boy, I was in the 4-H and the Boy Scouts. In high school, I played on the football team for two years until I realized that I was a better water polo player. So I gave up the gridiron for the pool. That's one of the reasons that I swam, because I loved water polo.

In college, the sport was my first love, and I'm proud of our team's success.

My parents were always there to support us children in sports, although they didn't force us to participate. My dad, Verne Scott, was always involved in booster groups, and now he and my two sisters compete in triathlons, too.

During my college years, I helped found the Davis Aquatic Masters Program, taking it from its original six members to more than 400 regulars before I had to leave the program to devote more time to training.

Even when I was in school, working with the Masters Program became a full-time job, and I look back on those days and the people I knew with fond memories. For awhile, I helped people who needed advice with their training programs, but I found that doing that kind of work didn't allow me enough time to meet my personal needs. It's always difficult to maintain some kind of balance.

Although I don't race just for the financial rewards, the fact that there is prize money is such an improvement over the way things were in the old days. I still race to be the best, and I train that way, too. I simply love to train hard—harder than anybody else. That used to give me problems. When I was in college, I would take pride in training harder than anyone else could. When I entered meets, I would race them like a workout. Sometimes I lost not because I didn't try hard enough, but because I was too beat up from hard training.

For the first couple of years after I realized this problem, it was still hard to let up a little in training. I was so accustomed to being at the starting line after having trained hard right up to that point, that it took some getting used to for me to back off a little before a meet. The years of training I've put in are another advantage for me—I've been racing, training, and working at sports ever since I was a little guy.

When I first learned about triathlons, back in 1979, it seemed like the perfect event for me. It wasn't so much that the three sports were swimming/cycling/running, but that it took all day to train to be great. It could be three different sports that take the same amount of time to train, the same endurance. I would have gone for it, because that is the part I love. I am driven to work hard.

WORKING HARD PAYS OFF

When I'm out on long workouts, I spend a lot of time thinking—and some of that thinking is about myself. A lot has been said and written about "Dave Scott, the private and solitary figure who likes to be alone." But that's just not who I am. I remember one magazine saying, "Dave Scott is a man commonly seen as an unshakable

Dave Epperson

Dave bikes 25–35 miles per day during winter training, increasing it in the spring..

monolith, as a mysterious and singleminded endurance maniac, immune to the petty insecurities that plague the rest of the mortal population." That's just not true.

I like people and enjoy being around them. Even more, I like to coach them. That's one of the things I really missed when I gave up serving as a Masters swim coach—the contact with people.

When I give a talk, I usually spend the first five minutes or so "warming up" the audience. I think I have a great sense of humor, and that is something you should share with people. I want the people in the audience to think of me as a person like them, to know that in most ways, I *am* like them.

ABC-TV, more than anything, has created this "Irontough, Iron-man" image of me, which has both helped and hurt me. When I line up at the start of a race, it can help because it can keep my competition from knowing what to expect. They may be thinking one thing about me, while I am thinking entirely different thoughts, not reacting to their image of me at all. I may wonder about the people who I compete against, but I know that the race is really me against my own expectations; I only have to compete against myself.

Sometimes, I have raced when I felt I was in terrible shape, such as the 1983 Bud Light Ironman. As we lined up on the beach, I said to myself, "It will be a miracle if you win this one," because I knew I just wasn't physically in condition for the race. Mentally I knew I had to be 120 percent.

I got out of the water in good position, and I knew then that I was in better shape than I had thought. I glanced over at my friend Pat, who goes to many of my races, and he nodded with that look that says, "There are eight more hours in this race, and you're doing great so far." Even so, that year when I finished the run, I couldn't focus when I crossed the finish line. I tried to wave my hand to the crowd, but I was trembling. It took all my concentration to run across that finish line.

Concentration is something I work on even in training. Because I train a lot by myself—not by choice necessarily—I have learned to discipline myself and my thoughts. I practice tuning in to what I am doing—focusing inward, translating that into action outward. I suppose that you just have to train alone a lot to develop that sense.

Knowing myself as well as I do helps a lot. I only compare myself against my own set of standards, not those of others. I have always thought that the Bud Light Ironman marathon times were slow for both women and men. Even though I hold the course record (2:53), set in 100-plus temperatures, I know we can go faster.

That is one of the drives that keeps me racing—I know that I haven't reached my potential. I know that I still haven't tapped just how good I can be, and I want to know that. That is what the moment of truth really means for me. I experienced it at the Nice Triathlon in 1984 when Mark Allen ran me down. Though I didn't take first place, I knew I had to face him in Hawaii in another month.

My day came at the Ironman, and I reversed the situation—he had a 16-minute lead starting the marathon. As I started the run, I just believed in myself. Though I would have settled for second that day, I took home the honors. I ran him down and won.

Dave Epperson

"I train to be the best."

It hasn't always been easy, but I have a burning desire to be the best in the sport. Maybe that is where the sense of fulfillment fits in my life. Fulfillment is a tough one for me, because I don't know yet what will satisfy my inner drive. That drive is powerful and I don't quite understand it myself. But I know that I want to be the most that I can be, and since I haven't reached that point yet, I will continue to compete and to find out.

Fulfillment for me isn't just about the triathlon. I've started writing a book—a training book that is really about a lot of other subjects—and in it I'll be able to share with others something of who the "real" Dave Scott is. I don't want to be known as just an athlete. I want to be fulfilled by everything in life, not just swimming, biking, or running. Triathlons are only a part of my life, not my whole life.

IT'S NEVER BEEN PRINTED

There has never really been a "Dave Scott Training Program," because I haven't written one yet. I have both studied and been studied as an athlete and advisor, and my educational, athletic, and coaching backgrounds have given me advantages.

Just how, and how hard, I work out depends on the time of year. I train hardest in the winter; that is, I train with the greatest intensity then. Once a week, I try to write a workout schedule, but how it turns out varies as the week goes along.

When people ask me how I train, I say that in the spring I usually swim three days a week at 5,000 yards, and two to three days at 3,500 yards, with one anaerobic threshold session that consists of long, intense work bouts—long intervals with brief rest periods, such as 250–800 yard repeats, with 5–40 seconds rest. After swimming I eat.

In the winter, I usually bike 25–35 miles at a time, increasing that in the spring. Three days a week, I time-trial 12–20 miles as hard as I can. The other four days I just ride or work hard on hills.

My running training has always been about the same. I rarely, if ever, run more than 14 miles at once. I've found that even at the Ironman, when I reach the half-marathon point, I know that I can continue at the same pace. My runs are usually in the 8–10-mile range, at a gradually faster pace until the last mile is at a five-minute pace or less. Twice a week I do mile fartleks with an eighth-mile rest. Again, this is my system of high workloads-to-short-rest ratios. Later in the season, the amount of rest gets higher.

Altogether, my weekly mileage averages about 30,000 yards of swimming, 275-plus miles of cycling, and 60 miles of running. That's what the other top triathletes are doing, plus or minus a few miles. But the amount of "training miles" doesn't correlate positively with

DAVE SCOTT'S TRAINING (SUMMARY)

Amount and intensity of training varies from season to season. In general:

Swimming: three days at 5,000 yards
two to three days at 3,500 yards
one anaerobic threshold workout, such
as 250–800 yard repeats with 5–40 seconds
of rest between

Total: 30,000 yards typically

Cycling: 25–35 miles per session in winter
12–20 mile time trials three days a week
distance or hill work other days

Total: 275-plus miles

Running: 8–10 mile runs, rarely more than 14 miles,
gradually increasing pace throughout the run
fartlek twice a week

Total: 60 miles

performance. Everyone can't train using the same workouts—we're all too different.

I like to finish my training and other activities by 6 P.M. so that I can have the remainder of the day for the rest of my life, my other activities. That's important to me: there really is a life other than training, and I like to share it with close friends.

Some things do alter my training schedule, just as is the case with anyone else. In my case, my relationships with my friends are extremely important to me, and there have been times when that concern has thrown my training schedule completely out of whack. One time in the middle of the season for example, I didn't train for nine days in a row. But I think of myself as being sensitive to others, and ups and downs like that are a part of keeping a balance I like to maintain.

That brings me back to knowing who I am and how I am different from others. Many people have advised me to move to San Diego and train with the triathletes there, in a more conducive environment. But I like the sense of the unknown that the competition has to face when I line up next to them. I enjoy that. There's a lot I don't want to reveal to people like Scott Molina, Scott Tinley, Mark Allen, and Kurt Madden—my weaknesses *or* my strengths. I like them

Dave Epperson

"There really is a life other than training and I like to share it with close friends."

always to be guessing. Because they train together, they know each other pretty well.

But I know myself, and I know that system wouldn't work for me at all. Even with all the reasons to leave, I won't. I like Davis. I prefer it here, with my friends, in my hometown, being who I am—Dave Scott.

*One of the balancing acts in triathlon is aboard a bike. Off the bike,
Sally Edwards uses these tools to coordinate commitments.*

11

MECHANISM 5

VIVACIOUS STRENGTH

As you move up the job responsibility ladder, there seems to be a direct relationship between the number of hours you spend on a telephone and the level of your salary. During one of those marathon phone sessions, George Cunningham asked me if I would speak at a Pacific Bell seminar. They were unfolding their *Blueprint for the Future*, a brochure outlining their plan for survival outside the womb of Ma Bell. George had reentered a Master's swimming program and was swimming faster than he had in college, breaking national age group records. The tools he used to attain success as a swimmer are also critical to success in the workplace, George said. Apparently Ma Bell, George, and I were all standing at the same crossroads.

Pacific Bell (formerly AT&T) was leaving behind a century-old nationwide phone system and entering the information age as a new and promising stand-alone company. Likewise, George—an animated, lively guy—was leaving behind ideas that he was growing older and slowing down. He learned from his sport experience to employ and develop his talent. You could take the Pacific Bell out of the corporate blueprint and insert the name George Cunningham; the corporation and man are headed in the same direction, and the methods they will use to reach their goals are essentially the same. Every successful entity operates on the same principles, whether it is a telephone company or a star athlete.

Pacific Bell's blueprint business plan is based on six commitments that express the values, the personal standards, and the sense of pride that the corporation wants to instill in its own employees. Pacific Bell's philosophy is that the success of the corporation rests on each employee's adoption of those commitments; if all of the company employees are successful individuals, the company as a whole will be as well.

We are customer focused
We deliver on the bottom line
We are creative can-do people
We value the individual
We communicate to get the job done
We are the best at what we do
Reprinted by permission from
Pacific Bell "Blueprint for the Future."

Pacific Bell may be in the business of delivering information while athletes are in the business of reaching their maximum fitness potential, but both use the same words in their blueprints: "high quality," "long-term growth," "financial needs." Some of the words are not quite the same. For example, though Pacific Bell says, "We are customer focused," the athlete would say, "I am [insert your sport] focused." The corporate world says, "We want to be the vendor of first choice," and the elite athlete says, "I want to be the athlete of first choice."

Pacific Bell talks about a "bottom line," which the company promises to deliver. This is the same line that athletes must realize in either their tangible or intangible net worth. The value of the sport must be worth the focus. Any kind of business must be profitable in order to succeed.

"We [Pacific Bell] are creative, can-do people." The world-class triathletes are made from the same successful corporate perspective, which relies on individual initiative and a far-reaching vision. Such a mentality recognizes that mistakes will be made and that they are a price worth paying for long-term improvement.

The final three stages of the commitment are: fostering individual success in people, prizing a leadership style that uses communication to achieve results, and, finally, a desire to be the best you possibly can. Again, these are the same tools champions employ to outperform their competition.

These tools and mechanisms are based on principles that are essentially the same in both fields. These principles or values direct and guide our performance as employees, athletes, or both.

The old rationale that athletic success is a function of good timing, talent, and a lot of luck grew out of generations of the slap-you-on-the-butt competitive mentality. But with the rise of the informed athlete, the new belief is that the achievability of excellence depends on your willingness to excel. It's possible that Pacific Bell's commitments might be corporate hype, all image and no substance. Even if that were true, the ideas are valuable, full of truth. The way you see through the smoke is by watching individual employees like George Cunningham. He is an example of the model in his passion to excel, communicate, and inspire others with whom he works.

To adhere to these commitments and to perform the required training will require personal strength. You must define yourself as an athlete first and as a parent, professional, or Indian chief second. The life of the triathlete is not a romantic one; it requires a quality of vitality, a commitment to consistent workouts over a long period of time, even though the disciplined athletic lifestyle can bring great joy to the athlete whose dreams are realized.

Many naturally gifted athletes must struggle to balance their lives and coordinate their commitments. Life doesn't stop during the training process; athletes must integrate their personal and professional lives, workouts, social and religious activities. Managing the whole is part of the overall commitment to excellence. It can best be practiced by adopting an attitude of vivacious strength.

As I stood in front of my Pacific Bell audience of 45 middle-aged women (and one man—George), each of whom had been promoted to middle management from the ranks of telephone operator, I finally realized why George had invited me to speak. One of his professional challenges had been to change the on-the-line operator's perception of her essentially mundane task—sitting for eight hours a day answering "411" calls. Many athletes find workouts equally boring—day after day of the same sweaty routine.

That night I spoke to my audience about each of them becoming a star. I said that each telephone employee can strive for excellence and—in Pacific Bell terms—be the best, a champion. George had invited me there to reaffirm the corporate ideology that everyone can become a hero unto him- or herself. In addition, with time, leadership, and accomplishment, each of us can become a legend. And that is the metaphor of sports. We can do it on a bicycle, in a swimming pool, running on the roads, *or* working for Pacific Bell. All forms of success are based on the same essential tools or values.

KURT ALAN MADDEN

Hometown:	San Diego, California
Date of birth:	September 15, 1955
Height:	5'11½"
Weight:	172 pounds
Maximum VO$_2$:	64 ml/kg/min
Body fat:	8 percent
Current profession:	Half-time professional triathlete and half-time community college PE instructor and cross-country track coach

Athletic achievements:

1980: Ironman Triathlon, seventh place

1982: Malibu Triathlon, sixth place
Pacific Crest Trail 50-mile Run, fourth place
Ironman Triathlon, sixth place

1983: Big Island Ultraman Triathlon, first place
Ironman Triathlon World Championships, tenth place
The Ultimate Endurance Triathlon, first place
Rio de Janeiro Golden Cup Triathlon, first place

1984: Bahama Diamond Triathlon, second place
Midwest Triathlon Classic, third place

Dave Epperson

Kurt Madden.

FROM ADVERSITY IN LIFE
TO EXCELLENCE IN SPORT

I was born in La Jolla, California, and moved to San Diego when I was four years old. My parents divorced when I was five years old, and my mother, who was a manic depressive, was put into a mental institution for a while. My father and I lived alone until he remarried when I was about eight years old. I admire my dad a lot because he really tried to be a good father and spend time with me as I grew up. He believed in the Puritan ethic—plenty of hard work and total honesty. He was a commercial fisherman, and every weekend we'd go out on the boat and fish together. I also had two half-sisters on my mother's side; they live with her.

When I was six years old, the doctors discovered I had a heart murmur and a faulty valve. At first they advised my father to keep me sedentary and very quiet, but several second opinions later, I was being advised to get plenty of exercise. I'd already begun to get that, because I was playing with the neighborhood kids and swimming and running with them, too.

We lived in a ghettolike area. I grew up with Chicanos and blacks

Dave Epperson

Kurt Madden prefers the ultradistance triathlons.

and picked up a lot of their traits and attitudes. When I was nine I was expelled from school for beating up another kid fairly badly. At that point I really didn't think about controlling my violent tendencies or see anything wrong in them.

I was fat as a child, but my body became more and more streamlined as I graduated from high school. At age 10, I started playing Little League baseball and Pop Warner football. I was also

Dave Epperson

Heading toward the finish line in first at the 1983 Ultimate below San Francisco's famed Golden Gate Bridge, Kurt Madden.

doing some pretty wild things during my evening hours with the neighborhood kids, but, luckily, I was never arrested.

When I was about 11 or 12 years old I began to realize what girls were all about, and because I knew more than my peers, I served as their advisor and directed them in various activities with girls. Consequently, I felt very respected and accepted. Also, I hung around with a lot of older kids, and I began to enjoy going to movies with girls rather than going fishing with my dad.

During high school, I played football and got caught up in playing the "macho man." I had to act tough there, because otherwise I would have definitely gotten thrown against a locker. In fact, in high school I learned that you have to act in ways that may not really be part of you in order to survive, so I would act crazy a lot of times, and then people would leave me alone. Basically, I played their game but kept out of things such as robbing liquor stores. During high school, after we played football, we'd drink and find girls. I'd always come home late, and that became a problem with my parents. It became such a point of contention between us that I decided to go to Long Beach and stay with my real mother.

In the meantime, my two half-sisters had gone in different directions. The oldest one got married at 17, and the other one became a prostitute at 14. She was heavily into drugs, including cocaine and heroin, and she murdered her pimp, Robbie Robinson, who was Sugar Ray Robinson's son. Although she escaped capture for four years, she was eventually caught and imprisoned near Los Angeles. When I went there to visit her one day, I decided to change the direction of my own life. The prison environment scared me so badly that now I would never even think of hurting anybody or doing anything that would put me in jail.

I decided as a senior in high school to live on my own. I lived with a few other guys, and once school was out I decided to work 80-hour weeks, which my father had always encouraged me to do, anyway. (Maybe I was a triathlete many years ago and never realized it.) When I came home from work I drank four to six beers until I fell asleep. I began to feel very bad about myself and was looking for a change. What really pulled me out of it was that I got hepatitis, and my grandmother died of cirrhosis of the liver because she was an alcoholic. I "retired" from alcohol at the age of 18.

After a complete reevaluation of myself and my goals, I started school at a junior college. Although it was a slow process, I gradually started coming back into focus. I got straight As and was determined to get a degree. I also started to run.

At San Diego State, where I was working toward a degree in physical education, I met Kelly. She was always intriguing to me; she had a certain air about her that I thoroughly enjoyed. I was looking for a more secure thing in my life, so we started dating regularly and, of course, fell in love. We got married in 1979 with a real commitment to making it work.

As I got into my education, I became more and more physically active and started to enter swim/run/swim races, especially Tom Warren's "Tug's" races. My goal was to win one of them, but the closest I came was third. Tom had won the Ironman in 1979; I felt that I could beat him. In 1980 I decided to go to Hawaii and try the Ironman, and Kelly really encouraged me. I came in seventh, and it really increased my level of confidence in sports. After that I tightened my training and really began to work on racing in triathlons. I continued my schoolwork and recently completed my master's degree.

I'm very emotional, and Kelly seems to have balanced out that aspect of me. She's very rational, so she helps me when I can't reason things out that way. I like to have someone to talk with on an intimate level, and Kelly is there for me. She's also tomboyish, so we can share a lot of different activities. She really motivates me

Dave Epperson

**Kurt Madden rides ahead of the lead vehicles at the
Bahamas Triathlon.**

because when I'm happy she's happy and vice versa. It means a lot
to me to know I'm racing for her as well as for myself.

I make an effort to be as positive as I can. I think it's important to
be enthusiastic and to come across as happy. People open up to an
attitude like that a lot more than to an aloof one. That's why I make
a deliberate effort to smile as I'm racing. It projects an image that
serves as a good example to others, one that perhaps they'll try to
project for themselves. Also, the spectators seem to give me a
similar return in friendly encouragement and feedback when I am
friendly toward them. I also try to be polite and treat other people
as I'd want them to treat me. I believe in being a kid when you're an
adult, and I still think I'm 10 years old in terms of being open and
spontaneous and vivacious.

My positive attitude isn't an innate quality. I certainly wasn't like
that five years ago. I've developed and reinforced it through my
athletic and life experiences. I push myself through adversity in the
most passionate way possible. This attitude also comes from being
a coach and having to play that positive role. As a coach, you have
to get your athletes primed and confident—not to the point where
they're overanxious but definitely to the point where they believe
they can run through a brick wall.

I'm determined because so many bad things happened to me as a
child. I didn't grow up in an encouraging environment, but despite

that I have found a good life for myself. I want other people to see that and realize they can escape their bad environments, too, if they're determined enough.

I feel I have a reason for living in wanting to help other people, and I'd like to write a book one day to encourage them or to feel that I've given back to the sport some of the things it's given me. I hate to see people make the same mistakes or go through the same problems I went through in my training or my life. I enjoy giving others some direction and guidance.

I get much more out of helping someone who makes an honest effort in what he or she is doing. Sometimes in a race I like to help by coaching other racers, but some take my advice and others don't. If I don't get any feedback, I shut it off; I don't push it on people. As a swim coach I might have 30 people in a class, and I'll concentrate on the ones who are really trying rather than the ones who are fooling around and aren't really concerned about improving. I want to "pump" the triers, and we'll usually have a fairly sound relationship because of that.

In turn, I really listen to and accept the advice of others, because my main priority is to learn and improve. To listen well, you have to have a positive attitude toward whatever someone says about you. You probably already know it deep down, anyway, although you may not have heard someone else say it. When you start to listen, you can make a more thorough evaluation of your progress and yourself as a person. It really adds to your overall discipline when you listen.

My motivation doesn't come from wanting to be number one. I operate from desire rather than fear, and I race against the elements rather than against the people around me. That's why the Ultimate and the Ultra Man triathlons intrigue me so much, because in both of them I have the attitude that no one is going to kick my butt, unless I do it myself.

I hate to see people come in second and behave as if they've totally lost. It's as if they're saying that all their training was worthless. They think of themselves as losers, and I think that's an awful attitude. You can finish second and be a winner. In fact, finishing second sometimes can be better than finishing first, because you're in a supporting role and push from behind.

I'm not losing my desire, but I am facing reality more and more. I don't think I was born with innate athletic ability. I think the reason I'm here today in triathlons is because I'm very determined, very disciplined, and I train really intelligently. I don't live in a daydream fantasy and say that someday I'm going to be the greatest, because I'm always going to be Kurt Madden. But I'm always going to wake up each day and do the best I can.

MADDEN'S TRAINING:
TRAINING IS TOUGHENING THE MIND

Because of my own education and all the coaching I do, I really understand my training and my body. I focus my training on certain races and make sure I recover. Each week I have goals, but they add up to an overall goal for a race. For example, if I'm racing in a triathlon in March, I might allow myself six weeks and label each one something like *easy, moderate, hard, hard, easy, easy.* My training for the Ultimate Endurance Triathlon really reflects my typical approach. The Ultimate consists of a 3.6-mile swim, a 153-mile bike ride, and a 50k run, so I train specifically for those distances. I usually increase my mileage on the bike from a recovery ride of about 30 miles all the way up to 200 miles and concentrate generally on increasing my time on the bike.

I take longer swims, from an hour to well above an hour-and-a-half and go a distance of 5,000 yards. In my training, I'll run the 50k distance at least twice on my own beforehand to develop mental toughness and to give me an opportunity to experience some things that I can then avoid on race day. I try to be really prepared for any race about 10 days before race day. During the last few days, I go through a lot of speed play and stretching, and, mainly, I get really psyched.

The same approach is true for the Bud Light Ironman. I'll practice the full race distance two or three times by myself before the race. Ideally, I will race in two or three Ironman-distance triathlons prior to Hawaii. Biking mileage 300–375 miles per week. Swimming will range from 14,000–16,000 yards each week, mostly intervals. As for running, I'll go from 4 miles of recovery running anywhere up to 15 miles.

I strongly believe that training by myself is best. I'm not really into the social scene when I work out, because I think I mentally toughen myself when I'm alone. When I go on a bike ride with a group of people it can sometimes mean two or three extra hours that I wouldn't normally be putting in, and it's two or three hours that I'm not sharing with Kelly.

I always swim by myself. I really don't need other people to motivate me because I'm just as motivated swimming against a clock as I may be against other people. I know what I have to do, so I just tell myself to get down to it and be tough.

If I want to get beaten up on the bike, I'll call Tinley or Molina, and that's good for me. However, many times, even if you bike with the best, if you go to the bathroom or get a flat tire, they'll leave you behind. They're so fast, they never stop, and if you get left behind, that's not good for your morale. But the same thing happens to

KURT MADDEN'S LOG

JUNE 1983

1—swam 4,000, timed a 500 at 5:48, ran 6 with surges, no soreness, legs responding to rest, bike 15, keep it smooth, weight 171.

2—swam 3,500, bike 15, ran 5, getting ready.

3—swam 500, ran 2, travel to Maryland.

4—swam 500, ran 3, bike 10 easy, race is tomorrow.

5—Oxford Triathlon, swam 4,200, bike 50, ran 21, 5th place, good job.

Totals: swim 16,200 yards; bike 125 miles; run 44 miles.

6—fly home, bike 20 easy, really sore and tired.

7—bike 40 on flats, tired jet lag, extra sleep.

8—swam 3,000, bike 30

9—ran 5, bike 100 to Oceanside (5:15), tough to get started.

them if they get a flat. An example of the kind of riding they do is a very long ride we went on last June. Twelve people, including Mark Montgomery, Mark Allen, Scott Tinley, and I met at San Diego Stadium. We had intended to do 50 miles, and it was an extremely hot day. I was equipped with a dollar bill and two bananas. The pace soon picked up. We ended up in the mountains—in a place called Ramona—about 60 or 70 miles away. The leaders wanted to go farther.

We continued to climb and got to about 5,000 feet, and the group decided to go even farther. No one admitted to being tired. We stopped twice for food and then had to come down from 5,000 feet all the way back to Mission Valley at sea level. At this point, there were only seven of us left. On our descent onto the freeway we just went completely crazy, and it was really scary because we went 40-45 mph down the hill, flat out. My legs were jelly three times over because the accumulation of lactic acid was so intense. None of us wanted to drop out first. I vividly remember that Scott Tinley was wearing a blue Ironman bicycle jersey that only the top 10 people get, and it was almost *white* with salt crystals. Altogether, it

10—ran 8, swam 200, shitty attitude

11—bike 40, bike 15, triathlete consulting.

12—bike 60, great, very strong, ran 8 solid.

   Totals: swim 3,200 yards; bike 305 miles; run 21 miles.

13—ran 11 moderate, bike 30 moderate, swam 4,000 moderate, 170 pounds.

14—bike 80, HOT, relaxed, worked on computer.

15—ran 16 great, bike 20 sore, swam 4,000 (4 × 1,000) 13:00, 12:53, 12:43, 12:34, weight 164 pounds, good day.

16—ran 5 (3 × 1 mile) 5:58, 5:49, 5:40 sluggish, bike 80 hard, stretching.

17—bike 30 fast, swam 3,000 continuous, ran 11, sore legs, stretching.

18—bike 40, time trial 10 miles 25:04, triathlete consulting.

19—ran 20, bike 40, mucho work.

   Totals: swim 11,000 yards; bike 320 miles; run 63 miles.

was probably about a 130-mile ride. In that situation, riding with others was actually good for me. You start to realize you can do almost anything you want if you can sustain yourself through an experience like that.

As far as running goes, I always run by myself because I like to run at my own speed, whether fast or slow. Nine times out of 10, when I run with someone else, I'm either half a step behind or half a step ahead, and that's not good for my mind. If I run a 20-miler alone, I can run at my own speed. I cut back my training on the weekends, so I can finish my training by 11:00 A.M. and enjoy Saturday and Sunday with Kelly. Some of the other triathletes aren't married, so they don't always understand that I don't want to waste time when I'm training! For them it's more important to do a 100-mile ride, even if it takes nine hours with stops for lunch several times along the way. For me, that's not quality time.

I don't use weights, although I tell myself I should. I just don't enjoy the idea of sore pecs, and currently I have only enough energy for swimming, biking, and running. If I ever got injured, I'd probably do some weight training.

Dave Epperson

Kurt runs from the swim to the bike transition area.

I'm trying to improve my diet to the extent that I don't eat one "hollow" calorie. My daily consumption ranges from 5,000 to 7,000 calories. When I'm not training I eat two meals a day, and when I am I eat about five meals a day. I go for a wide variety of foods with an emphasis on complex carbohydrates plus a lot of fruits, and I try to eat complete proteins. I avoid sugar and salt. My crutches are coffee and ice cream, which I think is common among endurance people.

I have a good nutritional background although I'm not a nutritionist, and I'm currently on the Phoenix vitamin plan, which consists of vitamins A, D, B, and C; I don't take megadoses. I also take digestive enzymes, and occasionally, if I'm feeling flat, I'll take a supplement of B_{15} and calcium.

One thing that I feel makes my training good is my common sense. I mean that, if I set my goals really high and I get three-fourths of my way through a week and I know I'm not going to hit them, I have sense enough to know I'm torn down or fatigued and that I should reevaluate some things. But my style doesn't work for everyone, so I think the bottom line is that you have to do what you believe is right for you. If you believe you should relentlessly ride up the coastline every single day, then you *should* do it because you have to have your own psyche.

His expression and his quadriceps both show the Kurt Madden commitment to vivacious strength.

INDEX